SALOME DEAR, NOT IN THE FRIDGE

Salome Dear
NOT in the Fridge!

Parodies, pastiches, gruesomes,
poems, satires, clerihews,
new nursery rhymes and cautionary tales,
odes, burlesques, eulogies, elegies, translations,
misleading advice for foreigners

all from the

New Statesman
Competitions 1955–1967

CHOSEN FOR THEIR BRILLIANCE, HILARITY
ORIGINALITY, ELEGANCE AND WIT

by

ARTHUR MARSHALL

London
GEORGE ALLEN AND UNWIN LTD

PRINTED IN GREAT BRITAIN
11 *on* 12 *pt. Ehrhardt type*
BY ABERDEEN UNIVERSITY PRESS

Foreword

For the benefit of the uninitiated, the *New Statesman* Weekend Competitions are weekly invitations to readers to show their literary skills in a variety of ways. Financial rewards await the most gifted. This selection of winning entries is the third to be published and it covers the period from the beginning of 1955 to the end of 1967, a highly productive thirteen years.

These competitions first began in *The Week-End Review* in March 1930. They began as they meant to go on and present-day competitors, wafted back nearly forty years, would find themselves quite at home. Competition No. 1 provided a choice of subject; there seemed to be a feeling, for there was a disparity in prizes, that the competitors would divide themselves up into First and Second XIs. For the bloods, the subject was 'A somewhat spritely prospectus of *The Week-End Review*', and among the non-prize-winners we find Edward Marsh (reproved for being non-spritely). The goats found themselves producing 120 words of purposely slovenly writing, the example given being 'Mrs Jenkinson closed the book. Then she heaved a profound sigh and placed it carefully on the dressing-table'.

From the first, the competitions had distinguished setters – V. Sackville-West, J. C. Squire, Humbert Wolfe, Dyneley Hussey, Lord David Cecil, Ivor Brown, Robert Lynd – and the subjects they then set are much as today: an epigram on The Ashes, a poem on Oberammergau, an Ode to Grape Fruit in the manner of Shelley, a Song Against Sussex, a love-letter from Pecksniff to Becky Sharp, Falstaff on a day at Ascot, entertaining names (Whalebelly, Trampleasure) from the London telephone directory. By Competition No. 4, the entries were 'many hundreds'. This was encouraging though the setters did not hesitate to be severe in their reports and, as early as September 1930, we find that, for dull and shoddy work all round, NO PRIZES at all were awarded – just a string of Dishonourable Mentions. Five years later, one competition ('Doodles of the famous') was considered so poorly done that *there was not even a report on it*. Did such strictures reduce in any way the number of entries? On the contrary. *New Statesman* competitors are made of courageous, durable stuff and the first request for clerihews

7

brought over 500 submissions. By 1932, there were as many as 760 competitors in one week, and by way of celebration a Competition Dinner took place in Gatti's Restaurant near the Strand (Tickets 5s, exclusive of wines).

Gradually the great names start to appear. April 1930 – Pibwob (First Prize) and Little Billee (specially commended), the latter advancing to a First Prize in the next month. In that December we find the name of dazzling R. J. P. Hewison. In 1934 the amalgamation between *The New Statesman* and *The Week-End Review* was achieved with no noticeable change of gears as regards the competitions (by now reduced to one subject only) and on January 27th there was printed a comment to remember: 'Allan M. Laing was another who began well, but appeared to get a stone in his shoe and finished limping.' He has limped to better purpose since. In October 1939, another landmark – Stanley J. Sharpless winning a prize for a clerihew on Gounod (you know); and three years later a breathtaking moment when the peerless L. E. J. won, with eleven others, a prize for 'the last words of an animal', moving quickly on to the first of that celebrated string of First Prizes. The delightful Nancy Gunter graced the scene first at about the time when the entries for Competition No. 510 blew out of Robinson Moody's bicycle basket and were lost for ever down High Holborn. But at least it was known what their fate was. Not so with those mislaid some months later by Roderick Random; as he confessed, 'Regrettably I have been true to my surname and the entries to the competition – how, when, where I can't imagine – have simply been lost'. Simply, indeed! The fact that at this time the war was in fullest swing is, like the entries, neither here nor there. First things first.

Once again, Honours Boards for the years under review are given here. The order of merit on them is a financial one. At the beginning of 1965 the prize money obtainable was generously increased (it will be recalled that Edward Blishen, bearer of a justly famous competing name, was once urged to spend part of his considerable winnings on a new typewriter ribbon). The setters, still mixing praise, encouragement and blame, have remained of much the same character, but with some different names. The main setters have been E. O. Parrott, Columba, Buzfuz, Hilbrian, D. R. Peddy, Malcom Shaw, P. W. R. Foot, Scythrop, L. Clarendon, Naomi Lewis, and the astoundingly gifted all-rounder, Martin

8

Fagg. Appearing now as Martin Fagg, now as Tim O'Dowda, now as Molly Fitton, prize-winners all, his rise from that first humble beginning (half a guinea in 1959 for a 'New Line in Winemanship') to competitor-extraordinary and most-prolific-setter has been unsurpassed. And we must not overlook the achievement of Peter Rowlett who, coming, as the race-commentators have it, 'from nowhere' in February 1964, went on to win no fewer than twenty First Prizes in that year.

To find that Martin Fagg is also Tim O'Dowda is to cast doubts on all names. What shocks are left to us? Is Allan M. Laing also Stanley J. Sharpless? Can Trooper Jones and Pibwob be one flesh? And what of those names which seem to be ingenious inventions – Perpy Traitor, Polly Glot, Norah Bone, Sawdust Asgold, T. Waddle? Genuine, every one of them? There is only one way to find out. It is time for another Dinner.

ARTHUR MARSHALL

Honours Boards

1955

Edward Blishen
H. A. C. Evans
Leslie Johnson
L. G. Udall
Little Billee
D. L. L. Clarke
Nancy Gunter
Allan M. Laing
G. J. Blundell
J. P. Stevenson

1956

{ Stanley J. Sharpless
{ J. R. Till
A. M. Sayers
Apple Tree
Leslie Johnson
P.M.
Rhoda Tuck Pook
D. R. Peddy
E. Timperley
{ H. A. C. Evans
{ Gloria Prince

1957

Gloria Prince
Stanley J. Sharpless
P.M.
Vera Telfer
{ J. A. Lindon
{ D. R. Peddy
Leslie Johnson
G. J. Blundell
Eileen Haggitt
D.A.J.S.

1958

Hilary
P.M.
Gloria Prince
Barbara Roe
Allan M. Laing
J. A. Lindon
Stanley J. Sharpless
Rhoda Tuck Pook
J. R. Till
C. W. V. Wordsworth

1959

Allan M. Laing
G. J. Blundell
J. A. Lindon
Gloria Prince
Nancy Gunter
Barbara Roe
R. Kennard Davis
H. A. C. Evans
Jeremiah Sowerby
{ Hilary
{ Rhoda Tuck Pook

1960

R. Kennard Davis
Stanley J. Sharpless
Allan M. Laing
Martin Fagg
J. A. Lindon
P. W. R. Foot
{ Lyndon Irving
{ A. M. Robertson
{ H. A. C. Evans
{ Trooper Jones
{ L. G. Udall

1961
R. A. McKenzie
Martin Fagg
{ Allan M. Laing
{ J. A. Lindon
{ A. M. Robertson
R. Kennard Davis
L. G. Udall
{ Miles Burrows
{ Trooper Jones
{ Peter Veale

1962
R. A. McKenzie
Martin Fagg
Trooper Jones
{ Russell Lucas
{ L. G. Udall
Peter Veale
Malcolm Shaw
{ P. W. R. Foot
{ Allan M. Laing
{ Stanley J. Sharpless

1963
Russell Lucas
Martin Fagg
R. A. McKenzie
June Langfield
J. A. Lindon
{ M. J. E. Burrows
{ Trooper Jones
Margaret Dunnett
{ G. J. Blundell
{ P. W. R. Foot
{ Nancy Gunter
{ Owl
{ Vera Telfer
{ Stanley J. Sharpless
{ Peter Veale

1964
Peter Rowlett
Russell Lucas
J. A. Lindon
Martin Fagg
Lyndon Irving
Peter Veale
John Digby
{ M. J. E. Burrows
{ Malcom Shaw
R. A. McKenzie

1965
Martin Fagg
Russell Lucas
Peter Veale
Peter Rowlett
Vera Telfer
Lyndon Irving
R. F. Leach
D. F. Juniper
J. A. Lindon
{ D. H. M. Cook
{ Denis Jolman

1966
Russell Lucas
{ Peter Veale
{ Roger Woddis
Tim O'Dowda
Martin Fagg
Geoffrey Minish
{ Bevis
{ L. G. Udall
{ Lyndon Irving
{ Peter Rowlett

1967
Russell Lucas
J. M. Crooks
⎧ Joan Fry
⎩ Peter Veale
Roger Woddis
T. Griffiths
Stanley Price
Martin Fagg
Malcolm Shaw
⎧ George Cowley
⎩ Harry Broadbent

Contents

1955

Going for a Song

(In the announcement of a sale of part of Bowood, the 'Big House' was already demolished into such component parts as doorways, panelling and architraves and 'Lot No. 288: The Entire South Elevation'. Competitors, borrowing styles from others, deplored this disintegration of the mansion)

SIR THOMAS BROWNE

From no enduring hieroglyph do we find, that particles of Pyramids were ever made the objects of common trade; or that Babylon's pendant gardens, as having outflowered their use, formed the stuff of diurnal trade. Rome suffered its Colosseum to stand, nor thought the passage of a few centuries cause for tearing down its applausive tiers. Pisa hath not peddled her tower; nor hath Venice deemed her palaces vendible. It is we alone who disarticulate great homes to please small dealers. Mighty mansions we sell piecemeal; ceilings go for a song, and a snap of the fingers buys the face of a fine house. When longevity is made a merchandise, who can say what shall scape the broker?

Edward Blishen

JOHN BETJEMAN

With a sandwich-lunch and a Thermos, we sat, Myfida and I,
On a mounting-block in the stable yard, as we watched the 'Big House' die
In the closing stage of a Golden Age 'neath a leaden Wiltshire sky.
Oh, the dealers and art-historians were having a *splendid* day,
(And the National Buildings Record man kept quoting the P.R.A.)
While the clock on the Barry Chapel was ticking our lives away.

'Going, a fine pine doorway! Come, gents, what am I bid?
'Going, a marble fireplace!' – (It's gone for a thousand quid!) –
And another load for the Brompton Road bumped over the cattle
    grid.

Oh, Farewell the South Elevation (Lot No. 288)
For a classical portico's 'no go' in a modern Welfare State,
Though a Windlesham broker's electric logs may glow in an Adam
    grate.

Then the clock struck six – and we shuddered, as mallet and crow-
    bar's thrust

Toppled the Marquess's pediment in a cloud of choking dust.
(But a bit of the kitchen-garden *may* go to the National Trust!)

Peter Clarke

What is this that Lights the Wigwam?

(*It was reported from Caughnawaga, Quebec, that a television aerial
had been erected in Chief White Eagle's wigwam in this Iroquois
village. Competitors described, in the manner of* Hiawatha, *the recep-
tion of the first programme*)

In the wigwam of the chieftain,
Gathered round the brand-new TV
Stood the sachems and the people.
When the screen first flickered brightly
Rose an Indian yell of welcome.
Silence fell upon the warriors
As they watched succeeding programmes;
Watched the jazz bands labour fiercely;
Watched the crooks and desperadoes;

Watched the endless advertisements –
And their hearts were filled with sorrow.
For *this* had gone the hard-earned mink skins,
The muskrat pelts, and all their wampum.
Up arose an angry murmur
Like a cloud of bees ascending.
With wrathful visage Chief White Eagle
Seized his war club, smashed it squarely
Down upon the grinning crooner,
Bringing peace unto his nation,
To the forest peace and quiet.

David Todd

To the wigwam of White Eagle
Hiawatha, Minnehaha,
And their bright papoose Lone Pylon,
Hied for Look-See-Television;
First they saw a weather-maker
Prophesying storm and tempest,
Then a newsreel and thereafter
'What's My Line?' and saw a spragster
And a batman's topper-upper;
In the interlude, the pausing
Watched a potter shape a vessel,
And debated on its purpose.
Best of all to Hiawatha
Was his aged nurse Nokomis
Catechised by Wilfred Pickles,
Cackling shrill with senile laughter
When he asked her, 'Are yer coortin'?'
Wending homeward Hiawatha
Vowed to write to Great Chief Pickles
For a Big-See-Television.

Nancy Gunter

Commercial Breaks

(Some well-known playwrights started their careers as advertising copywriters. Competitors imagined distinguished playwrights providing 'plugs' in dramatic form for ITV)

SHAKESPEARE

Canvasser: Good sir, be not mispriz'd upon mine errand;
      I would bespeak you as congenerous
      With our fraternity. Mark well this schedule.
(Shows him a Littlewoods football-pool coupon)
Citizen: I do, sir.
Canvasser: Nay, your pardon; 'tis as yet
      Unmark'd, but mark you, being mark'd aright,
      With due engagement to despatch your stake
      A sennight hence, 'twill fetch you argosies,
      And that sans parle or quillet. Stay, good sir,
      Set your charactery upon these dots,
      And you shall prove my words veridical.
(A week later)
Citizen: One X doth tread upon another's heels,
      And so my crosses make for me a crown.
      Ten thousand ducats at a cost of one
      This pool's no puddle; 'tis a springing well.
      O worthy canvasser, I give thee thanks
      For meting out that pregnant sheet of blanks.
      As narrow streams to mighty rivers flow,
      So forests vast from little woods can grow.

Leslie Johnson

CHRISTOPHER FRY

(An excerpt from *The Whites are White Enough*)

Husband: You recall to me lately
      My sainted mother when I was little.
      I refer to those eupeptic innocences,
      Those twin doves, her hands. She had
      Three maids, and never soiled them –

Her hands, I mean; nestling whitely
In her lap, or fluttering
The metaphysical air of her Thursdays.
Now I come to think of it,
You have begun to assemble
Conversible conversaziones, conducting them
With hands white as my mother's, or –
Come to think of it again – my linen.
Wife: How like a man! Marry us for what we have not,
And when we have it, praise us
Not for having it
By our own prudence, intelligence and housewifely economy
(We all use Daft now),
But for reminding you of your mothers,
White-handed at the expense of
The chapped, chopped, hang-nailed, discoloured and dis-
  torted
Fingers of the Abigails you
Would make of us if we let you.

R. J. P. Hewison

Who on Earth's That?

(Poems in praise of London statues)

THE DUKE OF KENT

The statue of the Duke of Kent
Is neither large nor prominent.
It occupies a modest space
On land adjoining Portland Place
And – quite against the normal course –
Is not provided with a horse.
So there he stands with books and scroll,
A dignified but kindly soul
Who – clothes apart – might almost be
A relative of you and me.

(The Legend briefly states that he's
Remembered for his Charities.)
So very few who see him there
Can know that one who has the air
Of no one in particular
Was Queen Victoria's Papa.

H. J. R.

GEORGE PEABODY

(who can be viewed in Threadneedle Street)

Peabody sits in Peabody's chair
Treating the City to Peabody's stare;
Who he was, what he was, no one could care
But I like to see Peabody there.

Noble in build as the Waldorf Astoria,
Deep are his roots in the reign of Victoria;
Passing, we hope, in a blessed euphoria,
Never for him was it *sic transit gloria.*

Magnate or Mogul, no proles will he greet;
Only the policeman on solitary beat
May see him, some dawn, rise to offer his seat
To the prowling Old Lady of Threadneedle Street.

London's stout pigeons make nonsense of Peabody;
Sometimes he wears in his hair a sleek wee body,
Preening and pruning and – oh what a free body! –
Crooning and croodling a love song to Peabody.

Catseye

NELSON

Dark tides of traffic slip
About the square's great ship;
But on that topmost mast
You stand for ever fast.

Black clouds in constant change
Above your proud head range;
But your eye holds in fee
The city's changeless sea.

And, farther, through a rift
Within the smoke-screen's drift
Would keenly scan again
The peril-haunted main.

Trafalgar, Victory, these
You brought from hostile seas.
Who signals, now, despair?
The blind eye still is there.

G. J. Blundell

Strange Bedfellows

(*Passages of dialogue from novels written in collaboration between two highly improbable collaborators*)

DAPHNE DU MAURIER AND NANCY MITFORD

"Rowena," I said, "I found this photograph in the second drawer of the bureau in the morning room, when I was looking for my will."

"Oh, darling, it's Edgar," she giggled. "Isn't he bliss in his coronation robes!"

"Were you married long?"

"Well, not really, darling, but then a day could be quite a long time if you were spending it with Edgar."

"In plain language," I said, "why did you marry him?"

"Well, he seemed a teriffic Hon. – *très gentil*. And then when he seduced me in the middle of my third season, Mummy thought it would be a good idea. So I did. Of course, he was awfully rich, and a Duke, but horribly middle-class – and not very nice, darling."

"I found these pills, too," I said: "There are seven of them – round, glossy, easy to swallow –."

"They're the sort you give to dogs," she said, "when they have to be put down."

"Rowena," I said, "was your first husband's death – accidental?"

She did not answer immediately. She straightened the rug over my knees. I saw that her eyes were full of tears.

"Oh, darling," she said, "why do Border Terriers have to get old and smelly?"

Gwen Foyle

AGATHA CHRISTIE AND ELIZABETH BOWEN

Poirot bowed courteously. "It is *très gentil* of you to come and see me, Mademoiselle," he said.

Felicity felt glad she was wearing the stole; somehow its femininity defied those very male moustaches.

"I had no alternative," she answered.

"But surely, Mademoiselle, the alternative was – *ne pas venir, n'est-ce pas?*"

"*Non!*" she replied sharply, deliberately asserting her own linguistic powers. "You see – if I had refused to come, it would have been somehow, as it were, a confession of failure."

"Confession! Then you confess, Mademoiselle? You killed your lover, *c'est vrai?*"

"Confess, kill, lover," she murmured. "You use these words as though they only had one meaning. But think how infinitely many gradations of meaning there are to the word 'lover' – ."

"Enough! Mademoiselle, I do not tolerate the equivocation. I, Poirot, ask you the straight question. Did you or did you not murder Roderick Spencer-Poumphrey?"

"Does it matter?" she sighed.

"Matter? *Mon Dieu!* Do you suggest, Mademoiselle, that Death does not matter?"

"Oh, it matters in a sense, yes. But compared with the slow weariness of life, with the subtle degradations of years in which illusions, faith, hope, are gradually stripped away – does it really, perhaps, so very much matter?"

L. W. Bailey

Created He Them

("Relentless in their pursuit of lust, avarice, cruelty, murder . . ."
Juvenal's sixth satire might today inspire rather different views on
women. And on men too)

ON WOMEN

This variant of Homo Sap
Is best considered as a Lap:
An ample, soft amorphous thing
Surmounted by an apron string
To which the male, as soon as hatched,
Remains despondently attached.
Its gleams of light are far and few.
It never thinks, but Always Knew.
Viewing all Nature with distrust
It chases particles of dust;
Abhors invention, cleaves to habit
And reproduces like the rabbit;
Allows its mate to work and sleep,
Refuses him the right to weep;
Delights to be considered frail
Yet normally survives the male;
However, as their lives are linked,
Will soon (V. Rabbit) be extinct.

Hazel Archard

ON MEN

A bane to flocks are wolves, far worse to lasses;
They roar about in motors, they make passes
And roam to seek the wretch who's easy prey.
Then there's the moral type in sober grey;
Assumed his sheep-like air: he hides, I fear,
A sharper tooth, worse tongue – get home, my dear,
Heed mother's warning – and her history.
And even so I'd lay she'd find a mystery
Th'advances made since Kinsey give the data.

'Twas bad form once to kiss and tell the mater:
One dropped a hint, but names were never said.
Today the eager scribbler, hot from bed
Tells all, feigns more: techniques, prowess. Apace
Comes Nemesis. How red the cheater's face
When Cynthia (smart girl with all the answers)
Grabs him all scared, and off to Brighton prances.
His poor display gives proof (an old, sad story)
His tongue, no other weapon, is his glory.

Canicollis

You and Me

(*Miss Nancy Mitford's adjectives 'U', indicating words and phrases
in use among the Upper Classes, and 'non-U' have passed into the
language. A dialogue between a U and non-U speaker was requested
on the news that the Duke of Marlborough had installed a milk-bar
for the use of visitors to Blenheim*)

U: You seem horrified, Mrs Flagorn. I think the new *buvette*
at Blenheim is a splendid idea.

Non-U: But a milk-bar, Viscountess – it's so common!

U: Not at all. I believe it's the first of its kind, though Lord
Fitzlarron and I are now planning to provide meals here
for our visitors.

Non-U: In this historic home?

U: In this very room.

Non-U: Beg pardon, your ladyship, but it doesn't seem right: a
snack-bar at Blenheim and this grand old lounge a cafe.
Fancy you serving dinners to trippers!

U: The staff would do the work, and we close to visitors before
dinner.

Non-U: Oh! But even lunches would be out of place here.

U: Indeed they would. However, by borrowing a little ducal
discretion we might contrive some – ah – light meals about
midday. Perhaps some of your Institute members could
help with the catering.

24

Non-U: Our ladies would be charmed, I'm sure.
U: You see, Mrs Flagorn, our plan has possibilities.
Non-U: Why, yes, viscountess! Fruit and greens from your
          garden; dainty serviettes with the Fitzlarron crest on them
          like your notepaper; there'd be hares and wild ducks from –
U: Thank you, Mrs Flagorn, for those valuable suggestions.
          Goodbye! Don't forget your gloves!
Non-U: Ah! On the mantelpiece. Goodbye! And many thanks!

Seumas

Ex Libris

(A Battle Song for a book borrower)

I am known as Dr. Jekyll, but I have a darker side,
As the kleptomaniac, bibliomaniac, book-purloining Hyde.
My better self, as Jekyll, is professionally chaste –
You'd never think, to look at me, that I was double-faced;
But when I get the urge to handle other people's books
The fingers of the surgeon change to predatory hooks!
As the kindly Dr. Jekyll I am often asked to pick
A volume that I fancy from the bookshelves of the sick;
But once within my bookcase, it is fated to reside
As a permanent addition to the library of Hyde.
It isn't that I can't afford to buy the books I read,
As the wealthy Dr. Jekyll I can purchase all I need;
But I gaze on my collection – and the devil's half of me
Whispers . . . " Such a lot of literature – and all acquired free!"

P. Nicholson

While John's books are profounder,
Tom's have more varied matter;
I therefore think it sounder
To carry off the latter.
I wander in to visit

For coffee at eleven,
Say, "That's a new one, is it?"
And leave with six or seven.

My promise is mere feigning:
I never do return them;
And he has stopped complaining –
I think he thinks I burn them.
Indeed, when he tried writing
To state his loss and ire,
His books themselves supplied my shelves
And his letters lit my fire.

Audrey L. Laski

The Giddy Limit

(*Rhymed curses on a breaker of the new (1955) Highway Code, be he motorist, bicyclist or pedestrian*)

MOTORIST

Scorcher, be you scorched as much
Firmly held in Devil's Clutch,
May the horn on which you sped
Sprout in two upon your head,
Catseyes filched from roadside pockets
Burn within your shrivelled sockets,
Roast in fire with none to dim it
At a speed that knows no limit,
Wail and hoot, and hoot and wail
Tail to Nose, and Nose to Tail.

Joyce Johnson

BICYCLIST

Pernicious Pest who loves to skim
Beneath my mudguard's very rim . . .
May your pedals and your chain

26

1955

Come detached on Salisbury Plain!
May a lorry vast as Titan
Block your view from Poole to Brighton!
Yapping dogs your legs pursue
All the way from Ham to Kew,
And when you're nearing Clapham Junction,
May your brakes refuse to function . . .
Juggernaut be at your heel –
And mine the hand that holds the wheel!

H. Vineham

PEDESTRIAN
(*a Mrs G. M. Hopkins*)

You, not waiting the Cross Now, bear
Your cross now: hate's hymn, your sin-song.
Silk-sacked shape, still simpering there,
Be blotch-mottled, skin-pimpled, long
Un-man-loved, miseried, maid-mocked, madam;
Be thralled by man-wolves, morselled into pangs;
Be chain-bound, stake-stocked, mulled in tar macadam;
Feed (O my God) fear's fell furious fangs;
Escape your inscape, be yourself unselved,
Your ghost-gathering, gloom-gaping grave's ditch delved
In a dreadful dingle. Then, tingle, itch,
Pitched on a prong unpitied in pit of pitch.

John Levitt

1956

Helpful Letters

(*Over-credulous listeners, believing that the Archers actually exist, are known to write to them, offering advice and ordering farm-produce. Other imaginary characters, serialised on the radio, might find themselves receiving similar communications*)

MRS. BENNET

Dear Mrs. Bennet,

Well done about Jane and Lizzie, also Lydia – my, that was a near thing! Mary next, and will be very hard, being plain and what is worse highbrow.

Nothing puts the men off more, they think of the joint burning and the nappies not washed, with her nose in a book. Music sometimes spells OPPORTUNITIES, and as she can't manage Light it will have to be Classics. But not Church or Chapel like accompanying the Vicar or Mothers' Union, people just think "Old Maid". She could teach it in one of those co-ed. schools, but if the men are the long-hair kind they don't always think on marriage lines. There's always the Colonies (though hard on Mum so far away, and you get rough types, oil technicians, etc.), but she would have to take up something portable, e.g., violin, pianos being short in the jungle.

Apple Tree

HAMLET

Dear Prince,

We heard your dreadfully sad news on the wireless and I am writing at once to let you know that if what they said was true and you are going to come to England as a refugee, we could easily squeeze you in at "Mon Repos" and pleased to. I daresay it is a

28

smaller place than you are used to at your Elsie something but less drafty also O you poor boy what a worrying time you been having first your dad going off so sudden then your college friend I suppose dressing up as a ghost and frightening you then your young lady friend going out of her mind and all and Im sure I don't wonder. We think it was those Russians again putting your Uncle up to dirty tricks. Now don't forget to send a p.c. to say when arriving Little Leoning is our station not much more than a Hamlet (ha! ha!) with you knowing our language so well already Im sure we shall hit it off fine together and our Glad is dying to meet you and show you round Give your Mum my regards we mustnt judge others must we.

R. M. Anthony

Strictly for Paedophobes

(*Poems Against Children. It will be remembered that Anthony Hope, emerging from a performance of* Peter Pan, *was heard to sigh "O for an hour of Herod!"*)

They ignore you if you're right, but they will blame you if you're
    wrong.
They despise you if you're weak, but they will hate you if you're
    strong.
Their logic is remorseless, but they don't know what you mean.
They're the enemies of order, but dependent on routine.
They will jeer at you, embarrass you, impoverish and flout you,
And for all you know they may grow up and write a book about you.

Barbara Young

Crocodile from Grey Towers, Ancient Seat of Learning,
Trailing down the avenue, pair by snooty pair,
With a cargo of snobbery,
Hauteur, prejudice,
Exaggerated accents and upper-class stare.

29

Arnold-haunted small fry from the local Grammar,
Standing in a huddle, waiting for the bus,
With a cargo of sniggers,
Spectacles, horseplay,
Brashness and Angst stemming from Eleven-plus.

Hordes of little bastards from the Secondary Modern,
Gadarening home to the Children's Hour and News,
With a cargo of comics,
Candy floss, ice cream,
Hollywood values and low I.Q.s

Stanley J. Sharpless

Birds Answer Back

(Our feathered friends reply to the poets who speak of them. In the case of Gray, it was "the moping owl doth to the moon complain")

THE CUCKOO TO WORDSWORTH

O noble poet! I have read
Twice through your eulogy.
You mean some other bird instead!
You surely can't mean *me*?

Such fine thoughts, it must be confessed,
Are shared by so few others.
You ought to hear the views expressed
By my dear foster-brothers.

And please omit this "fairy" rot;
I'm flesh and blood right through.
Or I shall wonder if you're not
A little cuckoo, too.

V. Rose

THE ROBIN TO BLAKE

I quite agree that Heaven must hate
The wire-encompassed robin's fate,

But never bird was penned in cage
Like men emprisoned for a wage,
Who forty years are daily seen
Immured within the seven fifteen.
Poor captive slaves, who all day long
Are cramped sans freedom, air and song!
And when the twilight falls again
They waste it, stifled in a train:
This mock of life from morn to sleep
Must make the hosts of Heaven to weep.

                                        Rhoda Tuck Pook

THE OWL TO GRAY

Who, who has dared to treat us owls so ill?
(With us, of course, it's U to use two whos)
To whomso'er it was, I take my quill
To twit him for his quite erroneous views.

Doubtless some elegiac poet grey
Too witless and too wooden in the head
To understand a whit of what we say
Has misconstrued my twilight serenade.

No, I do not complain, I'm not a grouse
(I do not give two hoots, when I am blue)
You heard me call my love to share a mouse
For that's our owlish way, to wit, to woo.

                                        F. Sinclair

Oscar and Bernard

(1956 was the centenary year of both Wilde and Shaw and, to celebrate it, each took a hand at re-writing one of the other's plays)

WILDE'S ST JOAN

Dauphin: Where do you come from?
Joan: A little village.

Dauphin: All villages are little; that is why they are villages. And as everyone leaves them they can't grow any bigger. Why have you come?

Joan: To help you.

Dauphin: When a woman says that she means that she will help herself.

Joan: And if a man says it?

Dauphin: A man never declares his intentions unless a woman makes him. Are yours honourable?

Joan: Yes. Will you give me what I ask?

Dauphin: That is what they all say.

Joan: Who?

Dauphin: All the women who come to Court. My wife doesn't like it. It takes an exceptional woman to appreciate her husband's generosity to anyone else.

Joan: Would your wife like to be a queen?

Dauphin: Of course. All wives think they should be queens; that is their illusion. Sometimes their husbands encourage it unwisely; that is their collusion.

Joan: Give me a horse and a suit of armour.

Dauphin: The others are more simple. They only want a carriage and a new dress. But perhaps you are subtler.

Vera Telfer

SHAW'S SALOME

Salome: Give that horrib!e thing to Mother. She asked for it.

Herodias: Darling child! As if I'd dream of killing your uncle's favourite prophet!

Salome: Not outright; yours is the roundabout method. And stop breathing maternal love over me. All I mean to you is another indirect channel for getting what you want. "The darling child will do this little thing to please her mother, won't she?" And you compel me to go on being a child because I wouldn't be any use to you as the woman I really am. You made me do that disgusting little-girl's dance in front of everybody this evening when by rights I should be decently veiled! Oh, I'm understanding you more and more. You daren't admit

to having a grown-up daughter because then Uncle
Herod'd know that you're quite old – nearly as old as he
is –

Herod: (*outraged*) Spank that youngster!

Alice James

Stop Me and Buy One

*(Poetic dithyrambs on wine, tobacco and food are legion but the innocent
delights of ice-cream have been overlooked)*

Kind ministrant to fevered lip and tongue,
Bringing relief from realms of ice and snow,
Modest, pale-featured nymph, by bards unsung,
Whose touch yet thrills, whose cold kiss charms us so!
Who has not seen you, in the sultry days
When raging Sirius bears the spirit down,
Coming – cool presence – through hot country ways,
Stopping to bless the parched and panting town?
Then, your white-fingered bounty knows no stint:
Then, ardent youth round your triumphal car
Sues for your flavours – chocolate, strawberry, mint,
Vanilla – and proclaims how sweet they are.
Melt not, chaste nymph! the frigider your kiss
The more we burn to taste its cooling bliss.

G. J. Blundell

Pale, wafered sweetness, cold and pure,
Cool salve to life's discomfiture!
This healing kiss, this chaste allure
Must tempt bright saints in the Azure
From thin ambrosial liqueur
To share such Treat of Gods, for sure . . .

Then grant, O Heavenly Epicure,
That when Thy Sundae Bell is rung
Thy "Come and get it" challenge flung,
I too may humbly queue among

C   33

The eager angels, old and young –
Our sleeves rolled up, our harps unstrung!
And when our joyful grace is sung
May I, with all the rest, give tongue!

P. M.

O Fat White Woman Whom Nobody Loves

(Frances Cornford's famous poem re-written with the key line 'O slim, dark woman whom everyone loves')

O why do your dresses all fit like gloves,
Hinting so much, and so much?
O slim, dark woman whom everyone loves,
Why do your dresses all fit like gloves
Over curves as sleek as the breasts of doves,
Moulding wherever they touch?
O why do your dresses all fit like gloves,
Hinting so much – ah! so much?

John Rhys

The policemen all are wearing white gloves,
And the Chairman smirks at the door.
O slim, dark woman whom everyone loves,
The policemen all are wearing white gloves,
And shepherd the crowd with pushes and shoves,
And you will arrive at four.
The policemen all are wearing white gloves,
And the Chairman smirks at the door.

Goodwill

O why do you garden without any gloves
Messing so much and so much –
O slim, dark woman whom ev'ryone loves,
O why do you garden without any gloves?

34

Your hands should be soft as the breasts of doves,
Not like a cheese-grater to touch:
O why do you garden without any gloves,
Messing so much and so much?

P. M.

Human Problems

*(Popular magazines often employ experts to answer their readers'
personal queries, a task which might have been undertaken by various
illustrious figures from the past)*

Question: When I was at the seaside last year my girl friend went
to the pictures to see Gregory Peck with my boy friend, just as
friends, but later they were unwise. Now a little friend has arrived,
and the question is whether he shall be named after my boy friend
or my girl friend's boy friend. We are all still friends. What do you
advise?

Dr. Johnson replies: Let the child be named for Peck. Circum-
spection in nomenclature will dissemble the vicissitudes of passion,
abate the counterclaims of sentiment, confound the inquisitions of
prurience, avert the censure of prejudice, harbour the redress of
reputation, indulge the diffidence of repentance, foster the emula-
tion of rectitude, and obtund the pungency of remorse.

N. S. Smith

Question: My husband prefers his allotment to me. Winter and
summer alike he leaves me alone in the house, to go and watch his
greens. Do you think this is an excuse?

Voltaire replies: Il me semble, chère Madame, que vous devez être
bien laide. Mais ne vous en désespérez pas. Vous pouvez toutefois
devenir une excellente pâtissière, et ce sera donc facile de faire
cuire un pâté exquis, y compris votre mari accommodé à la sauce
piquante et surmonté de tous ces légumes délicieux qu'il a si bien
cultivés dans son jardin.

Amy Hollins

Question: I am a widow with a thriving hardware business. A gentleman of independent means is courting me, but says I should first sign over the business to him. As he is young and inexperienced, would it be fair to burden him with it?

John Knox replies: You must complye and wouchsaif obediance. It wald be ane deuiatioun fra the propir ordour of Nature for ane wuman to rule ouir hir affeiris eftir Matrimonie, and like vnto slaverie for the man. Of late yeiris wemin haif socht to weare the breekis in mony spheuress of life to the confusioun of thame wha wald walk in Richteousnes. Dowbt not bott God sall recompanss sic malicious craft in thair awin bosome.

Seumas

Are You Sitting Comfortably?

(The television-set's views of its audience, in verse. These were almost entirely hostile and the competition-setter, reading the entries, began to have the uneasy suspicion that all the furniture in his room was watching him with loathing. And why not? Who likes to be eaten off, or sat on?)

With glazed, Cyclopean, exophthalmic stare,
I cast my spell upon the family,
Each member slumped in his accustomed chair
Or lolling comatose on the settee.

In two short minutes they are in my power,
Their blank white faces glimmering in the gloom,
Condemned for hour after grisly hour
To the unstirring silence of the tomb.

One night they'll fail to rise at programme's end;
"Strange TV Deaths!" the newspapers will cry;
The Yard, not knowing whom to apprehend,
Will not suspect the oblong Evil Eye.

Stanley J. Sharpless

"Morons and clots"
Says TV Kirk O'Shotts.
"Are they, by Jove?"
Says TV from Lime Grove.
"They make me cross"
Says TV from Holme Moss.
"Oh I don't know"
Says TV from Wenvoe.
"After all, they're our goldfield"
Says TV Sutton Coldfield.
"You're telling *me*!"
Says Commercial TV.

Nancy Gunter

A Rhyming Prophecy For 1956

(*Or, as it has turned sadly out, for pretty well any old year*)

Fog and snow for New Year's greeting, ban on all domestic heating,
Russia leaves an UNO meeting, threat of war in Middle East.
Feb. Australian Test team chosen, everything but wages frozen,
Eggs at two pounds ten a dozen, all war criminals released.

March – a scream for science teachers, eighteen horses fall at
    Bechers,
Oxford sink in Chiswick Reach as Cambridge win in record time.
April Budget, banks stop lending, Chancellor remains unbending,
"Money is not meant for spending", hire purchase made a crime.

Summer – one long string of crises, catastrophic rise in prices,
Thousands die from poisoned ices, crops destroyed by storm and
    pests.
Bread and meat go back on ration, fearful smash at Croydon
    station,
Living up to expectation, England lose the first four Tests.

Autumn Budget doubles taxes, U.S.A. and Soviet Axis,
Export wanes and Import waxes, Oval triumph – Rain. No Play.

37

Cabinet re-shuffle places, strictly on an Old Boy basis,
Same old names and same old faces; M.P.'s strike for higher pay.

Leonard Cooper

Disillusioning Glosses

(*Somebody has pointed out that Nashe's famous line "Brightness falls from the air" was in fact a misprint for "Brightness falls from the hair". Similar glosses were requested*)

Like one that on a lonesome road
Doth walk in fear and dread,
And, having once turned round, walks on
And turns no more his head,
Because he knows a frightful *friend*
Doth close behind him tread.   (Coleridge)

Leslie Johnson

As if this earth in *vast* thick pants were breathing.   (Coleridge)

Annie Allen

Strip no further, pretty sweeting.   (Shakespeare)

George Hurren

C'est Vénus toute entière à son *prix* attachée.   (Racine)

Esmé Kelly

Alone and *plainly* loitering.   (Keats)

Boothby

Whenas in *sulks* my Julia goes.   (Herrick)

J. T. Sharpe

The trivial round, the common *cask*
Will furnish all we need to ask.   (Keble)

Allan M. Laing

Nature I loved, and next to nature, *Art*.   (Landor)
("Art" was in fact the pet-name for a certain Arthur Williams,
son of a Cardiff butcher, the object of a romantic friendship of
life-long duration)

Dominick Salteena

Communist Boarding-schools

(*Mr Krushchev has announced that the Party proposes to set up
boarding-schools in Russia, for the first time since the days of the
Czars, "to produce good leaders". Various English applicants offered
their help and experience*)

DR ARNOLD

After much earnest consultation with the Almighty and in view
of the invaluable guidance I have been vouchsafed from that
enlightened source I conceive it to be my duty to offer my humble
services to do for Russia what I have already done for England.
Here my work is done, and now I will bend my energies to the
creation of a Russian Rugby, merely observing that it was not at
Rugby that the famous Battle of Waterloo was won, nor has the roll
of that celebrated establishment been sullied with the names of such
as Churchill or even Attlee. I beg of you to accept for the Republic
the Five Volumes of my Sermons which shall in some small measure
speak for me.

E. C. Jenkins

WACKFORD SQUEERS

If you want ennyone as can use the Cain I can ensure you I am
Abel. My Boys know how I lay on my marx and dont want telling
twice. The Boy at the Bottom gets the Boot. This is called learning
by eggsperience.

39

When I have done a Boy he is well Red, but I do not negglekt the Pragmattikal side. He can use a Hammer as well as a Sickel. On the Shop flore he will clere up enny forrin Matter.

My Wife knows how to keep a Bordy house, and sees to it that our Skollers are propper fed up. Every Boy is left in the State you want. Langwidge is no trubble. They soon lern the Words.

You say you want Leeders? You need have no feer. When I have done a Boy if he is not a born Leeder he is bownd to be an Iddyott.

Jim Parrott

Dejeuner Sur L'Herbe

(*The horrors of a picnic, in verse. The competitors, unbidden, chose various models*)

There are several reasons why a picnic is something at which
    I am apt to look askance,
And the least of them is ance.
Because the eventual discovery of a strip of sward that would
    brighten the eye of a Keith Miller or a Henry Cotton
Is almost immediately followed by a further discovery,
    i.e. that something has been forgotten.
And if there are picnic parties in which it is less common
    to hear a rebuke for forgetfulness than a gracious encomium,
Then shomium.
Furthermore, I prefer eating from a chair, be it tubular,
    contemporary or Windsor,
And I object to postures normally adopted by the kind of people
    who do their shopping on the Ginza.
So although I am dummer than my fellows in many ways,
    in one respect I am cannier,
And that is my aversion to the Thermos flask and the pannier.

Xico

Here I am, an old man with a dry mouth,
Bitten by flies among the cow-pats,
Eating dead winkles with a crooked pin.

40

And the end is the beginning, and tomorrow
It will be wasps at Runnymede. Last week
Lil had hysterics, throwing sandwiches
In the damp woods after a hard night's rain.
Here, on the waste ground behind the gas-works,
Gulls wheel and flock in the grey sky
Like the stones beneath an old man's bony buttocks.
I ache, much of the time, and long for winter.
O Vishnu, Vishnu (atishoo! atishoo!) – Lord,
Grant me a little peace before I die!
                    Mub! Eros! Llareggub!

                                        Gloria Prince

Picnic,
Hay-rick,
Flea, tick,
Neck-rick,
Tea thick,
Scones brick,
Jam-stick,
Wasp-flick,
Child sick,
Wet nick,
Home quick,
Colic.   P. M.

Tippler's Song

(*Of recent years, wines and spirits formerly only encountered in their
countries of origin have been brought into circulation. Topers commented
on this widening of their field*)

Before the Volga flowed to Rye, we drank our Beer and Gin;
The Brewers and the Gordons made the Flying English Inn.
In urban booths the roving youths plied maids with Nip and Dash;
In rambling shires the rolling squires sat Scotching Haig and
    Splash.

The Tio, it was Pepe, and the Cockburn, it was Red,
The night we went to Merrydown by way of Beachy Head.

We drank the Elderberry, and the Mead at Marazion;
We drank the Sussex Cider, and we downed the Dandelion.
But now the Vodka's in the Rye, the urban Bourbon's frappé;
In reeling shires they rock 'n' roll on Slivovic, Schnapps-happy.
But oh, my friends, there's still good Ale, and Bitter Beer and
    Sherry,
Before we go to Graham Greene by way of Bloody Mary.

                                              Xinna

Deflating Additions

(*Hilaire Belloc capped the virtuous Isaac Watts's line "Birds in their
little nests agree" by adding "With Chinamen but not with me".
Competitors made other lines of verse suffer in this way*)

It was not like your great and gracious ways
To stand before the window in your stays.

When you are old and gray and full of sleep
You haven't got to bother counting sheep.

                                        H. A. C. Evans

It is not growing like a tree:
In fact, I planted celery.

                                              Goodwill

Breathes there a man with soul so dead
Who was not, in the Thirties, Red?

                                              G. Moor

When lovely woman stoops to folly
The evening can be awfully jolly.

                                        Mary Demetriadis

42

1956

Yet once more, O ye Laurels, and once more,
I deliver the "Telegraph" under the door.

Edward Blishen

Full fathom five thy father lies,
His aqualung was the wrong size.

June Mercer Langfield

1957

Put it Away

(The pleasures of life have already been well sung. Competitors were asked to supply poems glorifying the joys of some form of asceticism)

CHASTITY

      Hail, Chastity,
That dams the primal fluid at its source,
Whereon, denied the channel Nature planned,
It spills itself in sublimating streams
To fertilise the ambient life of man;
Thus, Art, that baffles the appraising eye,
And Poetry, that sense and scansion lacks,
And Music, void of harmony and tune,
And Science, haunted by a mushroom cloud,
And Drama, ever looking back in ire –
All these, sweet Chastity, thou nourishest,
With that which else had served our brutish lust . . .

                          Stanley J. Sharpless

ABSTAINERS' DRINKING SONG

I always drink in company, I'd hate to have to carry
My liquor like a cactus or unsocial dromedary.
"Welcome! the drinks are on the house" will always be my motto –
Good cheer and bonhomie on tap, yet nobody gets blotto;
For it's not the drinks, my hearties, but the "Here's to yous" that
    matter,
And nothing keeps old friendships green like lots of lovely water!

CHORUS: Then come with me and we'll abstain
Where chlorinated waters bubble,
Together at the kitchen main
We'll see life whole and see it plain
And never, never see it double.

P. M.

TELLYTOTALISM

Let vegetarians delight
To celebrate their secret rite
With beans and vermicelli.
I have my own variety
Of social contrariety;
I have eschewed the Telly.

My ears unstopped, my eyes unglazed,
I'm not, like countless others, dazed
As mournful crooners moan.
My mind is not allowed to rust,
For, having had no Brains on Trust,
I've learned to trust my own.

F. B. Julian

Gruesomes

*(The invention of 'Gruesomes' has been a popular activity in the United
States. The classic example was:*
       *'Yes, yes, Mrs Lincoln, but, apart from that,
       how did you enjoy the play?'*
*Competitors supplied more, Marion Hill – to whom most grateful
thanks – supplying in addition a title for this anthology)*

Salome, dear, *not* in the fridge!

Marion Hill

How would you like your steak, Joan?

C. A. T.

Life goes at such a rush, doesn't it, Mrs Huskisson?

B. Mount

Mind my toga, Brutus; you splashed.

Stanley J. Sharpless

A pity, in fact, Mr Lot, that you have rather a sweet tooth.

D. R. Peddy

Bottoms up, Clarence!

Margaret Mylchreest

Tutelary Verse

(*For, in this case, the Prime Minister's country residence*)

CHARM FOR CHEQUERS

Comfort, Ease and Restfulness,
Be ye found in each Recess;
Dry rot, never take the floor,
Hence – all creatures that would bore!
Paths, be free of stumbling blocks,
Strike, ye clocks – and *only* clocks!
Neither blow nor knock upset
Any post or cabinet;
Every tap be leakage-proof;
All attempts to raise the roof
Utterly foredoomed and thwarted;
Bricks undropped, and bench supported;
All the mortars and cements
Made of strong constituents;
No division shall appal,
This the safest Seat of all!

Joyce Johnson

From the French

(Translations into English have proved a popular subject with com
petitors. Here they tackled Le Relais *by Gérard de Nerval:*

En voyage, on s'arrête, on descend de voiture;
Puis entre deux maisons on passe à l'aventure,
Des chevaux, de la route et des fouets étourdi,
L'oeil fatigué de voir et le corps engourdi.

Et voici tout à coup, silencieuse et verte,
Une vallée humide et de lilas couverte,
Un ruisseau qui murmure entre les peupliers,
Et la route et le bruit sont bien vite oubliés!

On se couche dans l'herbe et l'on s'écoute vivre,
De l'odeur du foin vert à loisir on s'enivre,
Et sans penser à rien on regarde les cieux . . .
Hélas! une voix crie: "En voiture, messieurs!")

One breaks the journey sometimes on a trip,
And dazed by din of wheel and hoof and whip,
Stiff and eye-weary, thankfully descends,
To go exploring where some short lane ends.

And there at hand, a valley – green and cool,
Offers its peace, – tall poplars by a pool,
A purling stream, the hedge with lilac gay . . .
And travel and the road seem far away.

One lies on grass, half-swooning in the sweet
Hay scent of it, and hears one's own heart beat,
Thinking of nothing, staring at the sky . . .
"Time to be moving" comes the unwelcome cry.

P. M.

On this oliday coach, like, was me and my pal
We kep belting along their Route Nashyional,
Fair chokka! The din, and yer backside that numb,
And this sight-seein lark, well, it's alright for some . . .

Well. These ouses we stop at. Like an alley between
We nip down, see, and Cor! At the end was all green!
Them tall skimpy trees on each side of a brook,
Not arf quiet! And them lilacs wherever you look.

It smelt lovely, real fresh, and we ain't said a dick
Just kerflopped on the grass . . . you could ear yerself tick!
Not a thought in yer ead, starin up at the light
Feeling soppy and appy just like we was tight.

The perishin trip all forgotten and gorn . . .
Till that bastard the guide started tootin is orn.

Esmé Kelly

The Consolations of Insomnia

(The pleasures and benefits of sleep have been hymned by many poets. Competitors – the vast majority of whom were female – wrote sonnets on the advantages of non-sleep)

What fools who, lying wakeful, number sheep!
Now I, once snug abed, am never bored,
Imagining all those perforce abroad
While I lie gloating – too content for sleep.
Who'd be on sentry-go when nights are raw?
A car revs up across the silent street
(The doctor, hauled from bed); come pacing feet,
The regulation bootfall of the law.
A foghorn! Middle-watch is tough tonight.
The lorry-convoys pass, and overhead
Plane engines throb, adroitly piloted;
Below, street-watchmen's bucket-fires glow bright.
I savour comfort, pleasurably stir,
Grin, flexing feline-wise, and all but purr.

Rhoda Tuck Pook

I Remember I Remember

(*Modern versions of Thomas Hood's poem*)

BEAUTY QUEEN

I remember, I remember
The year I won the prize,
The little judges peeping at
My bosom and my thighs;
I could not wear a stitch too few,
To show my winning form,
But now they've sent me back to school
To gym-slips and the dorm!

I remember, I remember,
The telly and the stage
Bombarding me with offers till
They heard about my age;
I've got to pass the G.C.E. –
It fills me full of spleen
To think I've got more subjects now
Than when I was a Queen.

Audrey L. Laski

TEDDY-BOY
(*To Gloria, from Jail*)

Wannit smashin', wannit smashin',
the dump where I hung out;
the Old Man use ter come 'ome cut
and knock me Mum about;
and last night's empties by the stairs
as up ter kip I goes,
and the tin trunk on the landin'
where I put me Teddy clothes.

Wannit smashin', wannit smashin',
the Palais and the Dive.
Remember when I done that bloke
fer askin' yer to jive?

D   49

and The Bug-'ouse every uvver night,
and fags and Dogs and beer.
I tell yer, I'm gonna Go The Lot
when I gets out of 'ere.

Tommy the Duffle

Don't Teach Your Grandmother...

(*Competitors submitted quatrains on transformed proverbs on the lines of the following, quoted from the Penguin* More *Comic and Curious Verse:*

Teach not thy parent's mother to extract
The embryo juices of the bird by suction.
The good old lady can that feat enact
Quite irrespective of the kind instruction)

BOYS WILL BE BOYS

The human creature of the male persuasion
Whose years come in the category "tender"
Will prove on every possible occasion
Youthful in age and masculine in gender.

E. J. Roberts

A CAT MAY LOOK AT A KING

No overweening monarch should expect
Immunity from feline observation.
The merest household pet may still select
The subjects its prefers for contemplation.

Oliver Coburn

ONE SWALLOW DOESN'T MAKE A SUMMER

Lone fork-tailed bird who fancied in thy pride
Thy soaring wings dispelled the year's attrition,
Know thou mayst quarter England's countryside
With not a gleam of sun in recognition.

Henry

HE LAUGHS BEST WHO LAUGHS LAST

Between the qualities of rival mirth
There is to be discerned a great disparity.
Priority in time yields place in worth
When measured against ultimate hilarity.

Leslie Johnson

Eeny Meeny Miny Mo

(*A Counting-out Rhyme for a Prime Minister picking his Cabinet*)

Mystery, history, call a consistory,
Cabinet gathering, gab in it, blathering,
Mustering, clustering, huddling, muddling,
Dreamers, seemers, schemers, triers,
Dabblers, babblers, gabblers, liars,
Flame-up, frame-up, flammery-shammery,
Jiggery-pokery, piggery-jokery,
Crookery-snatchery, cookery-patchery,
Clap-trap hatchery,

OUT GOES YOU!

Gloria Prince

1958

A Happy Occasion

(Newspaper reports and comments on the State Visit of the Queen of Sheba to King Solomon)

DAILY EXPRESS

The Queen of Sheba has visited King Solomon with a train of camels, bearing spices, gold and precious stones. In return she got all she asked for.

What is Britain doing? How much woad has been exported to Israel?

There is nothing to beat British woad. Yet other nations get ahead of us because we are too modest to boost our own wares.

Be proud of British woad and of the men who grow it and wear it. Remember that Solomon, in all his glory, has never been painted blue. He would welcome woad more than Sheba's precious stones.

Why? Because woad means the British way of life. Savages need it and we need the trade.

Let our coracles be loaded with woad. Let us sell British and buy British. That is the way to prosperity.

Bryce McNab

THE TIMES

Nothing but good can come of the visit of the Queen of Sheba to King Solomon. The tension between Israel and the Arabian states has long constituted a menace to the peace of the Middle East and only the intransigence and near-sightedness of previous rulers have prevented the solution of the hard question which formed a barrier to amity between Israel and her neighbours. Now wisdom, in the person of the King himself, has prevailed. Some, indeed, have looked with suspicion on the gifts exchanged between the visiting Queen and her royal host. But *timeo Danaos et dona ferentis* is an unworthy attitude to take, and nothing should be said at this critical time to denigrate the sincerity of the two rulers. There seems to have been complete understanding on both sides, and we see here a happy augury for future relations and one which may have far-reaching results.

R. V. Holmes

WOMAN

Yes, it *did* happen – a real-life Royal Visit with all the glamour and magic of a fairy tale. On an afternoon that glittered with sunshine ('Queen Weather', someone knowingly remarked), Her Majesty The Queen of Sheba arrived here to call on King Solomon . . . and set the crowds buzzing with the magnificence of her retinue. First came fifty camels laden with the most marvellous gifts – gold, jewels and spices valued at thousands of pounds. (Ever thought of keeping a camel as a pet? Make friends with your greengrocer first – camels are hungry creatures!) Then a long, long line of gay people from the entertainment world: clowns, jugglers, acrobats and musicians, all dressed by one of the world's top designers to tone with the occasion. And last of all, riding with matchless poise on an elephant, came The Queen herself ('isn't she *lovely*?' gasped our office junior), a regal vision in deep wine-scarlet and silver with headdress in citron-yellow to match her dusky complexion. Needless to say, we needed our hankies then!

A little bird told us The Queen had a lot of questions to ask The King once she had reached the Inner Sanctum. Knowing The King's reputation as a man of the world and businessman, we're sure he must have given some fascinating answers!

(By the way, how would *you* entertain The Queen of Sheba if she paid you a visit? Replies on a post-card, please, by August 31st – and the winner gets a lucky camel-charm bracelet!)

Pamela Sinclair

Triolets

(Competitors could choose any colour they liked for their poems)

Though fathomlessly black his eyes
    I will not wed Abdullah.
Though dark they are as Tyrian dyes,
Though fathomlessly black his eyes
They cannot win for me a prize
    For black is not a cullah,
Though fathomlessly black his eyes
    I will not wed Abdullah.

F. C. C.

The colour of bronze
    Denotes physical fitness.
You seldom find dons
The colour of bronze,
But mid-offs and mid-ons
    Will bear excellent witness:
The colour of bronze
    Denotes physical fitness.

Leslie Johnson

My subject is Gentian,
    A colour inviolate.
For a prize or a 'mention'
My subject is Gentian;
Bystander, attention
    To pun and to triolet!
My subject is Gentian,
    A colour in-violate.

Lyndon Irving

I wanted canary
    But this thing is mustard.
It is not a vagary
I wanted canary,

54

Like cream in a dairy
　　Or perhaps nearer custard.
I wanted canary
　　But this thing is mustard!

　　　　　　　　　　　　　　W. Parsons

A fine old vintage colour, puce –
　　But would one really wear it
Save for a waistcoat which in use
(A fine old vintage colour, puce)
I'm told hides spots of damson juice
　　Blood ketchup Bortsch and claret –
(A fine old vintage colour, puce)
　　But would one really *wear* it?

　　　　　　　　　　　　　　P. M.

Depressions

(*Lines from the opening stanzas of an Ode to Rain*)

Scavenge the gutter, rod the water-spout,
For Summer comes and June has busted out!
That cistern which we mortals call the sky,
Impatient, could not wait until July.
And thus, O humid goddess, I address
My ode a little late, I must confess.
And I would hymn the louder, if I could,
With all the zest of Barham and of Hood.
Thou midwife who, at birth, drown'st all my seeds,
Yet givest safe delivery to weeds;
Thou washerwoman of the ocean strand,
Who clearest fronts of kids and stop'st the band;
Of thee I sing, thou wet-bob's Alma Mater,
(I nearly said All Hail! but that comes later.)
Anglers' sweet handmaid, nurse of lakes and stews,
Who sendest rheum and floods to make the news . . .
　　Sixteen lines done; I write '&c'
　　Too bad; the weather has got wetterer!

　　　　　　　　　　　　　　W. G. Daish

How shall I bid you welcome if you never go away?
The warmest host grows chill at length with guests who overstay.
O for an island in the sun where you are never met!
Or even for an island where alternate days are wet.
I have spent many a summer – to give a farce a name –
Sitting goose-pimpled on a beach and wondering why I came,
And inched into that grey expanse the English call the sea,
And still the heavens opened, and still you rained on me.

Ninety-three million miles away the sun burns on in space,
I ponder on the distance as you drive into my face.
The Mistral and the Khamsin they blow both hot and dry,
And this, to me, seems worth the chance of sand in either eye.
I care not for Horse Latitudes, of Trade Winds take no heed,
The Beaufort Scale of Wind-Force I scarcely stop to read,
Of isotherms and isobars I little know or care,
But fluently can I recite the zones where you are rare.

Joan Ackner

I Controlled Margarine

(*The reminiscences of last-war combatants have poured from the press but there have been all too few personal chronicles from the home front. Competitors remedied this*)

from THE FULL AND THE EMPTY

This was our moment – the culmination of the long hours of waiting behind the blackout, the evenings spent endlessly rehearsing our manoeuvres till we could perform them instinctively. In the spare bedrooms the dummies were *in situ*; crouched in our appointed stations, we heard the nailed boots on the pavement outside, the harsh rap of the knocker. Calmly, Helen opened the door: as she did so, the stooping figures of the children flitted across the hall, ghostlike in the half-light. Climbing the stairs, our visitors passed them again, erect now and differently dressed. I switched on the concealed gramophone record of bath noises; the kettle whistled in the kitchen; footsteps sounded from the loft and the lavatory flushed automatically ... After the briefest inspection our visitors confessed 'You're choc-a-bloc all right – can't unload any more on you, can we?' and went on their way, declining even a cup of tea.

Hilary

from ARMS AND THE PEN

... but I achieved my finest hour while mobilising the English language, supplying a stylised terminology with evocative overtones.

Thus, in strategy, the 'pincers movement' recalled the handyman's toolchest, and 'bulge' anticipated the cult of vital statistics, kindling the imagination of the British fighting man. Psychological successes included 'points' (positive scoring rather than negative handicap), 'processed', with its scientific aura, and the simple Anglo-Saxon reassurance of 'Spam'. These I proudly acknowledge my own. My great grief was the official 'whalemeat' which, given imaginative nomenclature, could have triumphed, whereas – !

Consider the 'de-' group, -hydration, -contamination, etc., abstract polysyllable Latinities, contrasted with the chaste and gracious beauty of 'static water'. 'Firewatching', by its association with primeval forces, distracted countless minds from monotony and sordidness.

So, in service of my country and its tongue, I found my métier: this book has been just another joyous adventure in the traffic of language.

Rhoda Tuck Pook

from SWEET POINTS!

'It's for the kids', we explained, and everybody was most sympathetic and helpful. 'After all, it's not their bloody war', one woman said, and we agreed, marking her as a likely customer. 'It's for the kids', we told the paper-manufacturer and he supplied us with exactly what we wanted at once; I think he was only sorry we weren't in the note-making trade. We put him down. 'It's for the kids', we explained to the printer, who seemed at first inclined to jib. 'What have they done to deserve Hitler?' we asked indignantly, and though he sweated and kept looking at the door he finally agreed to come in with us. On the strict understanding that he was to have nothing to do with it, of course. 'It's for the kids', we explained when people noticed how much we were taking. They usually had kids of their own.

Gloria Prince

Secretaries' Day

(September 30th, 1958, was, apparently, Secretaries' Day, and inspired various bosses to leave notes in the typewriter to greet their willing, supposedly, slaves)

FROM A CABINET MINISTER

Your loyal service, dear Miss Smart,
Has deeply touched me in that part
Which private members call their heart.

Through Agriculture, Health and Food,
Your double-spacing matched my mood.
You brewed the tea, while others booed.

And when I nearly lost my seat
By asking Randolph in to eat,
You put the poison in his meat.

Accept this M.B.E. and grade
As Personal Assistant (Trade).
You'll understand . . . the post's unpaid.

Guy Hadley

FROM A HEADMISTRESS

Miss Binks! – or may we make it 'Binkie' now
That we've so many school suspenses shared?
The day our plumbing went all anyhow,
The night we found the San, with sheets unaired,
The breakfast-beetles in our Quaker Oats,

The hockey-match when Matron went berserk,
The Parents' Meeting where I lost my notes
And muddled Jenny Boote with Jessie Burke,
The Prefects' Riot when we raised the hem –
(By Jove, those gels can fight! We never knew.)
All this brings back the little apothegm:
Omnes eodem cogimur – and you
The foremost, Binkie, of our pioneers!
This is Your Day; and though we break a rule,
Tonight in Hall we'll give three rousing cheers:
Oh, *good* old Secretary to the School.

Pamela Sinclair

FROM A BIG BUSINESSMAN
(in appreciation of willing service)

Dear – , your favour 7th ult
While giving cause for satisfaction
Did not forecast this net result
Outwith the terms of our transaction.
The increased figure you now mention –
Less coverage – I need not say,
Will have considerate attention:
I shall indent for your outlay
Until such time as your decision
To take delivery or no
Requires some adequate provision
Consistent with the *status quo*.
I trust you will approve this scheme
And know how anxiously I wait
The further proof of your esteem –
Not, may I hope? in duplicate.

P. M.

Home Cooking

(Songs in praise of any cooked dish. If the competitors are any guide, the distinguishing marks of NS readers are, suitably, plain living and high thinking)

PAELLA

Estella, Estella, they're cooking up Paella
Down in old Valencia among the orange trees.
Señoras and señores, Don Pepe and Dolores,
Are seated round the copper pot with plates upon their knees.

Refrain
Paella! Paella! Arroz by any other name would never smell as sweet.
Paella! Paella! Every Spanish girl and feller
Takes it by the spoonful, every belch is tuneful,
Takes it by the shovelful to give themselves a treat.

Estella, Estella, you're sweeter than Paella,
You're cuter than the octopus, the chicken or the fish.
It's true I love Paella, but you come first, Estella,
After you, Estella, Paella is my dish.

C. W. V. Wordsworth

SEMOLINA

Allow me to praise Semolina;
I thrill to its pallid off-white.
There rarely, if ever, has been a
Milk pudding so utterly right.
The P.Gs., I grant you, are keener,
For instance, on gooseberry fool,
And when I was younger (and greener)
They'd get what they liked, as a rule.
But now that I'm wiser – and meaner –
My fat bank account's my reward,
So three cheers for sweet Semolina;
I don't have to eat it, thank Gawd!

Norah Bone

COQUILLE ST. JACQUES

Good St. Jacques, rest content; did you really invent
This most succulent poem in fish?
I'm not often this keen on anything piscine,
But here is my dream of a dish.

For with one humble scallop (or two), plus a dollop
Of fat, and some onions and herbs,
Behold a repast that's but rarely surpassed
And no normal digestion disturbs.

You can keep tongues of larks, the prepared fins of sharks,
Turtle soup and smoked salmon as well.
There's a sturgeon in roe? Let her stay down below;
Here's a banquet in one single shell.

D. R. Peddy

Blessed and Hallowed

(*Verses on the English Sunday*)

After the City churches and the Dome
I would suggest you choose a quiet seat
On a bombed place and there compare the beat
Of London's pulse with yours; or scrape a comb
Or rusted chisel from the dust of Rome;
Or trace the earthed-in course of River Fleet;
Or simply tramp the streets on tired feet;
Or else go home and sleep. You have no home?
Then, stranger, come with me; you shall eat beef
And apple-pie; and taste with me the grief
Of that remorseful, downward-sloping bend
Which on Time's chart tails off our grey week's end.

Margaret Dunnett

The milk arrives, the papers come; there isn't any post.
The morning, for an English Mum, turns on the Sunday roast;
While visiting aunts go off to church, and vicars call the banns,
And Fathers polish up the car and the kids walk down to Gran's.
And much of Monday's wash goes out, and dinner's after one,
And somebody else but Mother goes and gets the dishes done.
The city spills, the country fills, how *Sunday* looks the sea!
Fresh cakes are made, a clean cloth laid, the boy friend comes to tea.
And after seven, spades hung up and mowers roll away,
And wheeling flocks in cycling socks are bound to get home today;
And dusk comes down on weary lines that crawl in from the coast,
And Monday breathes in the larder cold, congealing the Sunday
      roast.

Hazel Archard

Mind Your Q's and P's

(*Extracts from a book on Etiquette for the Animal World*)

from ETIQUETTE FOR THE DISCRIMINATING CAT

. . . when the meal is to be served, the occasional purr appassionato tremolando is permissible, and one may rub oneself discreetly against the Caterer's legs. But do not overdo it: plaintive mewing is to be eschewed. As milk is being poured, keep the head well out of the way, and the paws out of the saucer. Lap slowly from the edge and spill as little as possible. Nowadays a plain bowl is preferable to those non-U ones marked CAT, DOG, PRESENT FROM WIGAN or, worse still, BABY.

Should the Caterer proffer anything *cooked by herself*, leave it, tactfully, down the garden for those revolting strays. That should teach them. You may remedy the consequent calory deficiency by a makeshift, self-service snack, say, a mouse *surprise* or a bird *natur*. This should be taken, not in the house, but running-buffet style.

James S. Fidgen

from COURTESY FOR COBRAS

1. It is always permissible to offer apples to a lady, but not to a man. Let the lady persuade him if necessary.
2. When assisting a queen to commit suicide, bite deep at the breast or it may be necessary to call in a confrère to attack, say, the arm. (Asps please note.)
3. Aquatic serpents may assail Trojan priests, but it is advisable to finish off the children as well in case they seek revenge.
4. If an adder wishes to multiply, it should do so by logs.
5. If captured and deposited in a wicker basket, it may be necessary to sway and gyrate to the public amusement if your captor places a pipe to his lips, despite the hideous sounds which emerge.
6. To boas: if placed round a lady's neck, constrict her.

B. Sabine

Cautionary Tales

(*Rhymes for present-day children*)

Thomas, an Air-Marshal's son,
Loved to push the neighbours' bells;
Laughingly away he'd run
Heedless of their angry yells.

Tom, when visiting H.Q.,
Found a red one labelled 'GO.
WARNING' (underlined in blue)
'Please don't press till Ike says so.'

Saint Peter with a startled look
Drew a line and closed the Book.
'See,' he said, 'what comes of boys
Playing with their father's toys.'

A. W. Clarke

The chiefest of young Ethel's vices
Was eating multitudes of ices.
Whene'er the ice-van's booming tinkle
Was heard, Eth ran out in a twinkle,
And gorged herself on large 'Vanilla';
Her Mum foretold that it would kill 'er.
No tears could thaw her; once she ran
Away, and hid inside the van,
And promptly froze upon the spot
Like the saltpillar-wife of Lot.
Poor Eth is licked! Behold the follies
Of one whose lolly went on lollies.

Gerda Mayer

Poetry for Portraits

(*Rossetti used to append sonnets to his pictures and competitors were asked to produce verses, not necessarily sonnets, for various familiar portraits*)

WHISTLER'S MOTHER

Sez Ma Whistler to her Jimmy-boy, 'See here now, son, sez she,
'You've painted Limey bridges, but you ain't done painted me.
''Bout Art I don't know nothin', but I know what I prefer –
'Git out your paints and brushes for the Picture of the Year'.

'Aw, shucks', sez Jimmy Whistler, 'do I really have to, Ma?
'I never went for paintin' things that look just like they are.
'Think what those darned Pre-Raphaelites would say' – but
    'tweren't no use;
When Ma had made her mind up she'd throw out the best excuse.

His artist pals proclaimed it was the best they ever saw,
But none could recognise it as a picture of his Maw,
And up until they guessed it, to inquirers he would say
'It's called Old Lady Nocturne', not to give himself away.

Norah Bone

64

JOHN'S MADAME SUGGIA

Gazing upon this canvas, we recall
A figure borrowed from an antique frieze,
Sublimely heedless of who hears or sees,
Held captive in the unknown music's thrall.
The virtuoso of the concert-hall,
The dark, high-cheekboned, scornful Portuguese,
Playing with effortless, majestic ease,
Lives here for ever. Yet that is not all:
Evoking the response of eye and ear
Both interwoven to a single strand,
The ghost of some Bach melody seems near,
Caught by the magic of the painter's hand,
And in the fusion of two arts we hear
The grave perfection of a saraband.

Geoffrey G. Riley

Clerihews

(*The Clerihew has always been a popular exercise with competitors. Here they are on famous beauties in history or fiction*)

Of Dorian Gray
People would say:
'When you're nearer acquainted
You'll see he's been painted'.

Said Nell Gwynn,
Of original sin:
'Any chap'll
Take an orange instead of an apple'.

Hardy Amies

'Not again for a fiver!'
Confessed Lady Godiva.
'You'd never believe how much a horse itches
When you're not wearing breeches'.

E   65

I'll bet a tanner
That when Susanna
Got caught among the trees the one that held her
Was an Elder!

Livingstone K. Bluntmore

Salome
Wasn't what you'd call 'homey',
Her dish for a feast
Was *Tête Baptiste*.

Joyce Johnson

Emma
Was in a dilemma
When her hero, with all his charm,
Cried 'Come to my arm!'

Little Billee

That Narcissus
Should acquire a missus
Was an idea that he rejected
After he'd reflected.

Norah Bone

In the Beginning

(*To correct the erroneous notion that the great* end *of poetry is rhyme, competitors were encouraged to write a poem, entitled* In the Beginning, *with initial disyllabic rhymes*)

Darker the night of chaos than we know;
Starker its bleakness than our minds can grasp;
Hidden the shapely universe until
Bidden to revelation by the Word.
Wonderful then the rolling ball of Earth
Under the cruising lights of moon and sun;
Flower and grass entrancingly arose,
Shower and sun inciting them to grow;

66

Creatures began to stir, to run, to flaunt
Features which generations would endorse.
Vastly creation's panorama spread.
Lastly emerged the name-bestower, Man.

Audrey L. Laski

Maybe the milky fragrance of young creatures –
Baby and calf and puppy – was Creation's
Odour, the breath of new-born things whose sweetness
Flowed o'er the earth. That scent grows faint, we barely
Savour it now, our jaded senses rather
Favour the aura of man's own inventions.
Flower and growth have lost their smell of wonder –
Power hath emanations more enticing,
Drugging the mind. 'Tis in brief moments only,
Hugging some soft young life, we breathe the primal
Essence, and go more humbly to our Science
Lessons, whose end is but decay – and stenches.

P. M.

Long Farewells

(*Two unregretful good-byes*)

BISHOP

Farewell, you Deans and pious chaps
Whom I have known in aisle and apse;
Your faces, names, without regret,
I'll soon conveniently forget
When from this dark and damp cathedral
I fly with arms outstretched, dihedral.
No more the dreary press reports
Upon my hasty, uttered thoughts
About the cat and AID
And skirts that end above the knee.
Relieved of gaiters, mitre, crozier,
I see my future brighter, rosier.

Lyndon Irving

BUM

Im aleavin this henouse forever
With an hobos farwel on the door
Ive et som togh chickens but never
Had poultry so stringy before
The drafts come from hunderds of notoles
An you caint git no rest on the floor
Where it aint muck its bumps and wet potoles
An you keeps wakin up stiff and sore
Ive had the bumsrush from spekeasies
An foxoles for beds in the war
But I rackon sheds cold as deepfreezes
Is a downrite insolt to the poor.

W. G. Daish

1959

The New Stateswoman

(Printing disputes and take-over bids may one day result in the amalgamation of the literary weeklies with the women's weeklies. Competitors provided extracts from regular features in such a magazine)

HINTS FOR AUTHORS-TO-BE

These months of waiting can be the happiest months of your life – and there is no need to think that automatically you will be unattractive, moody and irritable. . . . Remember, there is nothing unnatural about writing a book. It is no longer regarded as something to be hushed up . . .

Visit your local library regularly and talk to the librarian – he is there to help you. He will advise you what to read during these months and rest assured that he knows what he is doing. Modern literary skill and methods are always available for every expectant author nowadays.

When the appointed day draws near, don't panic. Begin to collect your explanations and excuses so that you can go straight to the publishers . . .

And what joy will be yours when at last you hold the tiny volume in your hands.

G. Morley

WILHELMINA STRONG'S QUIET CORNER

It's getting near election time, that gay MP-selection time, when X means more than just a kiss; a chance that you must never miss of sending back to Westminster the sort of members you prefer. Mr Macmillan looks just right – distinguished and oh, so polite. His Premium Bonds are just the thing to get our savings into swing. Yet every wise girl ere she picks, thinks back to 1956 and then recalls –

forget who can? – Macmillan was a Suez Man. But Mr Gaitskell's Labour boys will give us Welfare and its joys – free milk and orange juice galore, and council dwellings by the score where HE can come back home to you when his long working day is through. And when your tots are older you'll send them to Comprehensive School. So girls who dream of life sublime will vote for LABOUR every time.

D. R. Peddy

STATESWOMAN TO STATESWOMAN

While punting on the Isis the other evening after a Summer School at Ruskin for Redbrick lecturers in social anthropology, my friend told me he found *Das Kapital* unreadable. What should be my attitude? – Madge.

Your friend sounds a bit obtuse to me, Madge. Of course the book's not so un-put-downable as *Lolita* (God, how I loathed it at Girton) but he's simply writing himself off as a political square if he can't make an effort – if only for your sake. If he talks like that about one of the half-dozen really seminal books of all time, how are you and he ever going to make a real go of things together? Remind him of the Webbs. Of course, as his mistress (you are his mistress, I take it?) you could always try Lysistrata's tactics of disengagement, and see how that worked – Aunt Critica.

Stanley J. Sharpless

Mnemonic

(A rhymed mnemonic of the 40 counties of England)

Lying south of sweet Northumber
Lands of Westmor, Rut and Cumber,
Nottingham for forest walks,
Durham, Derby, Lancs and Yorks,
Leicester, Warwick, Wilts ahead,
Fords of Here, Staff and Bed,
Shires of Lincoln, Shrop and Ches,

Sexes – Middle, Sus and Es!
Worcester, Gloucester, down the Severn
South to Somerset and Devon,
On to Dorset, Kent and Surrey
Passing London in a hurry.
Berkshire Thames where Oxford punts,
Herts or Bucks for Cambridge Hunts,
Hants and Northants, Norfolk, Suff,
Cornwall, Monmouth – that's enough.

Donald Monat

Is It That You Comprehend?

*(The words of a folk nocturne by Janacek were translated into English
on a record sleeve as follows:*

*'A poor mother scraped to bring up her son Johnny.
Now he must leave her and go to a distant land.
"Where is your hair, Johnny?" asks his mother.
"They shore me of it by the River Danube." (i.e.
he was conscripted and had his hair cut.)'*

Other examples of Translators' English were requested)

FRANKIE AND JOHNNY

Frankie looks through the hole in the key and there notices her
Johnny on the couch-bed being very affectionated with Nelly Bly.
He was her sweetheart, but he was behaving to her very improperly.

Allan M. Laing

THE DRUNKEN SAILOR

Wearing a tubular trouser the offender shall be placed in the
drainways when the dawn bursts. Urah! and the lady springs from
bed when the dawn bursts.

Livingstone K. Bluntmore

71

AULD LANG SYNE

> Is it that elderly bosom pals should be overlooked
> And not fetched to the brain?
> Is it that historic cronies should be obliviated
> And epochs of old-fashioned heretofore?

Stanley J. Sharpless

BILLY BOY

> A dote-mother beseeches her boy 'Where did you all day?'
> 'I did all day spending with the charming Nancy who so
>   teases my imagination,' he tells.
> 'Can she cook a goulash of sheepsmeat and earthapples such
>   as the folk of Ireland eat?'
> 'Yes,' he assures, 'and a special sort of sweetcake as in
>   Lancashire too.'

L. G.

Nearer God's Heart

(*Poems 'In Dispraise of Gardens'*)

> On a new estate, between gravel and clay-ground,
> At the suburb's edge, between field and town,
> Walled round with brick like a prep-school playground
> Is the ghastly garden that gets me down.
> There's a heap of stones, that we call 'the rockery',
> And a tangle of tussocks we term 'the lawn'.
> In the poisoned earth of the rosebed's mockery
>   Toadstools spawn.
>
> The soil is strewn with the builder's rubble,
> The briars grow bold and the brambles bind.
> The neighbours gather to watch my trouble
> And tender advice that is seldom kind.

72

..

1959

Bottles and boots and broken kettles
Gleam in the gloom of the blossomless bed,
And under the wall, in a nest of nettles,
                          Cats lie dead.

                                  R. Kennard Davis

Of grass I've had my chlorophyll
It grows here all for lawn
No blade cuts blade; the mower's still
Since palms have grown a corn.

Go to, thou ant, thou slug who bide
In wait for root and stem
And fatten on insecticide
And know no requiem.

I have no heart for fork and spade
Or sprays that kill the grubs
And wilt to hear those compost talks
Dished out to gardening clubs.

Nay, Babylon was firm and just –
No sentimental pardons –
No mercy for her angry dust –
She hanged her bloody gardens.

                                  Lyndon Irving

Children's Dictionary

(*Robert Graves once quoted the following definitions from a dictionary for children, compiled by Anna Brownwell Murphy about 1810:*

    TO ABANDON, *is to leave or go away from; an* abandoned *man or woman means a* very *wicked* man or woman.

    TO ABHOR, *is to hate, to dislike very much indeed*; *as* 'God abhors liars'.

Prizes were offered for words and definitions equally flavoured with current assumptions about morality and suitable for a modern children's dictionary)

73

FRIEND, a very close acquaintance indeed, as in '*We are just good friends*'.

TO EXPEND, is to spend or to consume. To get a meal *on the expenses* (noun, pl.) means *to dine very liberally*.

Anne Hathaway

CAPITALISM, is a game in which anyone can win but only those with *money* ever do. It is a *good*, *healthy* game for all children.

COMMUNISM, is a game in which no one wins and those with money have it taken from them. It is a *nasty* game and is only for grown-ups.

C. D. Throsby

DELINQUENT, slightly naughty in a trivial way; as 'The delinquent child, who set fire to a church, was told not to do so again'.

DIVORCE, the friendly parting of married people; as 'My mummy has promised me a new daddy when she gets her divorce'.

Vera Telfer

ADOPT, to take from someone else: to choose, e.g. If a child is adopted, this means he was chosen by his parents, and not just an accident.

Winifred Joyce Taylor

CHRISTIAN, an enemy of the State who, in olden days, used to be thrown to the lions, e.g. 'There was an extra lion, so one poor lion got no *Christian*'.

Chauve-Souris

KEEP, have charge of, maintain, not lose. A *kept* woman is the opposite of an *abandoned* woman (qv).

Hilary

TO LOVE, is to like very much indeed; a *lover* is a very special boy- or girl-friend who may not be married yet, but perhaps ought to be.

Allan M. Laing

RELATIONS, those connected by birth or marriage. It is good to have relations, but not relations *with*; that is often bad.

P. W. R. Foot

HUMAN, belonging to mankind. 'Only human' means cheating, lying, etc. on a small scale.

David Burnard

SOCIALISTIC, unfair, not very honest; a person who tries to take something that doesn't belong to him or wants to *change the rules* is *socialistic*.

Henry Walter

Sans Wine

(Competitors commemorated the centenary of the publication of Fitzgerald's version of the Rubaiyat by composing a message from Omar Khayyam to the world of 1959)

The Centuries, with mingled Woes and Fears,
Roll on and bring but sad Increase of Tears:
The Poet-Singer, peering from his Tomb,
Rhymes not with Hope the last Eight Hundred Years.

What Worth your Flying Ships and Iron Ways
When Care on every Brow a Wrinkle lays?
Your Hakims banish Pestilence and Pain,
But War, the worst of Pestilences, stays.

Gaily your Scientists accept their Load
And travel heedlessly the fatal Road:
With tireless Zeal they search Earth's Secrets out –
Their Aim? To make the Universe explode!

Take Heed: if that last Rocket shall go up,
Think not with Omar in the Shades to sup!
For such as You Heav'n's Vintner has prepared
The last frustration of an empty Cup.

Allan M. Laing

75

Streams of Consciousness

(The rambling thoughts of a Parliamentary candidate during the chairman's opening remarks at a public meeting)

Glad to welcome candidate me. Madam Chairman, committee-woman busybody. Not bad body, actually. Careful. Concentrate on audience who all know me she says. Chap in third row, nasty customer. Cauliflower ears. Planted by opponent. Cauliflower plant. Proliferating proletarian plant. Quatermass monster. Quatermasses of people demand sound statesmanship. Men of stature. Chairmadam of stature, not bad at all. Perhaps time for few questions after. May I ask one question, Madam Chairman? Careful. No breath of scandal. Clean fun rather. Make 'em laugh. Gaitskell-duggery. Bevans alive! Uproarious. Brings much-needed wit to Westminster. Captivates Madam Chairman. Careful. Steady now. Nobody wants listen chairmadam all want hear candidate. Hear hear candidate. Clap clap open my trap. Madam Chairman . . .

Peter Veale

Ladies and gentlemen? – there they are all right, though only Sam – thank heaven for agents – knows where they come from or why – whose interests are henceforth *my* interests, like the foundry-men's interests yesterday, the farmers' this afternoon, the rate-payers' tomorrow – but they don't believe me, do you, you wizened witch in the first row with your eyes popping – you'll know me next time, ma'am, or is my fly unzipped? – Parliamentary Candidate On Exposure Charge – that'd *really* set me up as a Prominent Local Figure, pledged to support my constituents on Crucial Issues – though what Issue could be crucialer than when do I get my beauty sleep? 50 per cent don't know and 50 per cent don't care, provided I bring to this job those sterling qualities etcetera, as though you need any qualities in this job beyond a set of warm underclothes and a taste for starvation. Politics? Oh come, let's keep politics out of this . . .

Hilary

I'm Trying To Give It Up

(Tobacco, once hymned by Calverley and others, is now under a cloud.
A song was asked for, for or against 'the weed')

God made the good tobacco for a solace and a boon,
And the man who speaks against it is a rascal and a loon,
For whether it's a pipe, a cigarette or a cigar,
Tobacco spells tranquillity from Maine to Malabar.

The Choctaws and the Cherokees just hated the police,
But when they finished scalping them they smoked the Pipe of
    Peace,
And subtle Orientals, most inscrutable of guys,
Are fabulously fumophil and wonderfully wise.

Our boys are seldom junkies and they don't go on a jag.
They'd rather drink a glass of beer and smoke a quiet fag;
And see our greatest Englishman, the pattern of the breed,
Enjoying his twelve inches of the wonder-smoking weed.

So here's to Lady Nicotine, the fairest of her sex,
Who eases torn and jangled nerves with comforts multiplex;
Beneath her spell the gravest threat becomes a harmless joke,
And plots to ruin continents go up in clouds of smoke.

H. A. C. Evans

1960

Sharpeville

(*The massacre at Sharpeville took place in March, 1960. F.C.C. were the initials of Frances Cornford*)

No vine of hatred sprung from seeds of now,
Fruit black on every bough;
No monument white future hands may rear,
Each chiselled name
Perpetually clear;
No Mea Culpa in distraction said;
No present shame
Can ever hide away
The sprawled and innocent dead,
The happened day.

F. C. C.

Modern Industrial Processes

(*Factory procedures in verse in the style of Dr. Erasmus Darwin, to whom is here allotted an extremely posthumous first prize*)

ARKWRIGHT'S SPINNING PROCESS

First, with nice eye, emerging Naiads cull
From leathery pods the vegetable wool;
With wiry teeth revolving Cards release
The tangled knots and smooth the ravell'd fleece:
Next moves the iron hand with fingers fine,
Combs the wide card, and forms th'eternal line;

Slow with soft lips the whirling can acquires
The tender skeins, and wraps in rising spires;
With quickened pace successive rollers move,
And these retain, and those extend, the rove:
Then fly the spokes, the rapid axles glow
While slowly circumvolves the labouring wheel below.

E. Darwin

COLD-WELDING TWO ALUMINIUM STRIPS

First are the Coated Tongues of silver-grey
Fed to the high-speed whirling Wires which flay
The surface with their steel, rip off the dross,
And leave a mutual-joy reflecting gloss
On mirror'd Lady Metal and her Match.
Now hold, moist panting breath! Hot fingers, snatch
Not with such greasy appetite at Love,
Till Married properly by Force Above.
Cold-press'd with Applicable Tool together,
Both in one Die, the upper on the nether,
No more to separate in peace or war,
The pair now barely half of what they were before.

J. A. Lindon

THE HYDROGEN BOMB

First gentle cordite goads the massy sphere
With twin of Pluto's silver to cohere:
Now wingéd neutrons pierce the sacred door,
And two appear where one had stood before;
This lightning army grows to set ablaze
The soft Deuterium with ardent rays.
More swiftly yet, shy Protons now unite
And sacrifice their limbs for greater light;
And new-born Helium with zealous flares
Outshines by far the sun whose name it bears.
The surging orb soars heavenward and dies,
While gaping riven Earth stares feebly in surprise.

G. J. Stirling

79

Rather Cross Purposes

(Conversations on the Wolfenden Report in which the first speaker thinks the subject is the Report on Sport, while the other thinks it is that on Prostitution and Homosexuality)

A What do you think about all this money being spent on amateurs?

B I must say that I didn't read that in the report. But it's certainly made the game tough for professionals.

A Not really. They've got their own resources; very highly paid most of them are too.

B But they've got to play for safety all along the line.

A Don't worry. We'll always have them. We must keep up with other countries. Wolfenden's seen the red light.

B Good heavens! You don't mean state control? The public would never stand for it.

A Nothing so drastic. Just getting together men with a common interest and encouraging them.

B Look, old man. I'm sure he didn't say encourage.

A Well, he meant it. And I'd rather spend money on that than H bombs.

B The lesser of two evils. You may be right. But *I* didn't get that out of the report.

Vera Telfer

A I don't think we do nearly enough of it in this country.

B You surely can't mean that you want your son and daughter to indulge in such activities.

A Why ever not? They have always been extremely keen at school, and taken part vigorously at every opportunity. They must get that bursting energy out of their systems somehow.

B But it will be the ruin of this country as it was of the Greeks!

A Nonsense. The Greeks led the world in it as our country has done until lately. I should like to see the authorities spend far more on facilities for improving our proficiency in these matters; my husband and I have always been enthusiasts ourselves, believing that Nature intends our bodies to be properly and enjoyably exercised.

Monica Sherwood

If Not

(Kipling's If re-written to conform with the spirit of the times)

If you can't trim your sails to suit the weather,
If you can't take your chance to pass the buck,
If you can't offer cardboard goods as leather
And then persuade the mugs to buy the muck;
If you can't work a profitable fiddle
Or cheat the Customs when you've been abroad,
If you can't wangle your returns, and diddle
The Income Tax, yet not be charged with fraud;

If you can't learn the craft of social climbing
And damn the eyes of those who're underneath;
If you can't kid your friend you're not two-timing,
Then, when it suits you, kick him in the teeth;
If you can't run a car on public money,
Or have your lunch each day at the Savoy,
You're going to find that life's not all that funny,
For, take my tip, you'll miss the bus, old boy.

H. A. C. Evans

I Polished Up That Handle

(The following appeared in The Times *personal column:*
    'Titled persons interested in being appointed a director of a sub-
    sidiary in Great Britain of an International Group should write
    giving full particulars in strictest confidence to the Managing
    Director . . .'
Replies came from some unexpected quarters)

LADY CATHERINE DE BOURGH

I am the Lady Catherine de Bourgh. You will, of course, require
no further information, and I am graciously pleased hereby to
signify my acceptance of the directorship you offer.

I will delegate my chaplain, a Mr Collins, an honest, reliable sort of man, to collect my fees when he is next in town. Kindly send bank-notes to save my foot-men the trouble of washing coin.

G. J. Blundell

LADY BRACKNELL

My reply to your notice in *The Times* is prompted by the fact that you do not disguise yourself as a Box Number – a device offering opportunities for the concealment of social indiscretions equalled only by the cloakroom. Lord Bracknell is obviously the person you seek. As he has never been permitted to express an opinion on any subject whatever, nor, in fact, has he ever indicated a desire to do so, he is admirably fitted for the appointment. He is, I am glad to say, quite uninformed on matters of commerce.

I require satisfactory answers to the enclosed questionnaire before proceeding.

P. R. B.

UNCLE MATTHEW
(*Nancy Mitford's* LORD RADLETT)

One has to be broad-minded these days, dammit, so I'll come in – provided you don't expect me to waste my time fussing about indoors with little bits of paper; also that the board does not include any of the following: Frogs, Wogs, Wops, Jews, Jehovah's Witnesses, Huns, Homosexuals, Poets, Papists, Mormons, Musicians, sewers from Oxford or the British Council, Stockbrokers, Yanks, Niggers, Beatniks, Bankers, bloody Russians, Dissenters, Dagoes, Women, Trade Unionists, Cubans, Actors, Plymouth Brethren, Picasso, Psychiatrists, Commies, Colonials, those Congolese swine, etc.

I have no objection, of course, to *normal* people.

Martin Fagg

Oranges and Lemons

(1960 *versions of nursery rhymes*)

'Like, pussy cat, pussy cat, where is you was?'
'Like, I was at Beaulieu to get all that jazz.'
'Like, pussy cat, pussy cat, what happened there?'
'Like, if you don't know man, you must be a square!'

Michael Myer

'Pussy cat, pussy cat, where have you been?'
'I've been to London to visit the Queen.'
'Pussy cat, pussy cat, what did she say?'
'Something beginning My Husband and I . . .'

R. A. Peacock

Bar! Bar! Black sheep!
Have them in our school?
No Sir! No Sir! Ah'm no fool.
One for the white boy, and one for his Jane,
But none for the nigger boy who's plantin' mah cane.

D. M. Jowett

Hey! diddle-diddle,
The Stock Exchange fiddle,
The bulls jumped over the bears.
The stockbrokers laughed
At such lucrative sport,
And the take-over boys got the shares.

A. J. Ryder

Ouch!

(Competitors were asked to compose a threnody on a Dying Plant, Flower or Vegetable after hearing that a researching horticulturist has announced that plants are sentient beings and suffer the pains of dissolution in much the same way as human kind)

MIMOSA AFFLICTA

What, lying, Mimosa?
What, dying, Mimosa?
Your bipinnate leaves hanging limp –
Our cocker-pup knocked you and shocked you, Mimosa?
The imp!
He larked, poor Mimosa?
And barked, poor Mimosa?
What pain to a sensitive plant!
Great Gardener tend you and mend you, Mimosa –
I can't.
Naught serves, poor Mimosa;
Your nerves, poor Mimosa,
Have suffered a fatal collapse.
No hope! You must lie there and die there, Mimosa,
Next life to enact as a cactus, Mimosa,
Perhaps!

Gloria Prince

DIRGE FOR THE DANDELION

O piteous sun,
Torn from thine emerald sky,
Thy shrinking rays grow darker, one by one!
Bare roots, like entrails, twitch in agony,
Toothed leaves decay,
And from cracked stem thy milk-blood leaks away.
No more from thee
Shall puffing children learn the time of day!
Few weep to see thee pass:
Though toddling infants crowed
To snatch thy golden mintage from the grass;

And, with a happier end, thou might'st have glowed
In cottage cup
As golden vintage; or made leafy sup
In poor abode.
Alas, as wretched weed they pulled thee up!

Doris Pulsford

Give Me Your Answer Do

(Leap Year proposals that didn't quite work out)

ELIZABETHAN DRAMATIST

Volumina: ... O pretty youth, O super-dainty youth!
   His arched brows, his hawking eye, his curls
   Are meat for lusty bawds. By God, I'll have him.
Slender: Save you, fair lady. Keep you comfortable.
Volumina: Marry, so I mean, sweet Joseph, in thy bed.
   Myself am moved to woo thee for my husband.
Slender: Now, by Dian, I am too young for you.
Volumina: Out, whey-face! You are as a tallow candle,
   The better part burnt out. Virginity
   Is but the cowish terror of thy spirit
   That dares not undertake. Your self-abuse
   Is the initiate fear that wants hard use.
Madam Trull: Whip thee, gosling. 'Tis a cold thing, a very
               stockfish.
Volumina: I must needs have him with a codpiece then ...
   Nay, by the Mass, he's fled.

(From *'Tis Pity He's a Stockfish*, by Beaumont sans Fletcher)

Trooper Jones

HENRY JAMES

And though I was in understandable dubiety as to what – when
she Oh! so beseechingly whispered, 'Could you conceivably, do
you think, bring yourself to consider a very delicate proposition?' –

she was precisely 'up to'; the, alas, so wary bachelor in me, ignoring the innocuous possibility of, let us say, a dinner party, precipitately took fright and, one cautious eye on the calendar, uttered with sudden firmness the pardonable exaggeration – 'I deeply regret that I should find myself *in every imaginable way* at present, dear lady, "*booked up*"!'

A. M. Sayers

Adjust Your Seasonings

(*The witches in Macbeth did pretty well with the nasty ingredients for their cauldron. What might modern witches use?*)

Ear of blackleg, hep-cat's eye
Ravished when the moon is high.
Pinch of fall-out, pint of smog,
Whisker of a Sputnik dog,
Shred with lock of murderer's hair
Singed in the electric chair,
Gooseflesh from a nudist's flank,
Nostrum brewed by nature crank.
Nose of nark, and thumb from fist
Of a quack psychiatrist,
Add a test-tube infant's caul
Minced with anti-Semite's gall,
Hoodlum's disc that slipped when clout
Laid an aged widow out,
Sprinkle quicklime, stirring fast,
For a garnish at the last.

Rhoda Tuck Pook

Into concrete mixer throw
Brick from shoddy bungalow,
Thrice three chunks of orange peel
Gathered from the beach at Deal,
Foot and hare untimely slain
On the outer traffic lane,

Cast-off paper from a toffee,
Cup of instantaneous coffee,
Then, with fag-end torn from lip,
Sexy film and comic strip,
Nucleus of hydrogen,
Thousandth egg of battery hen,
Paint-brush used for marking wall,
Thoroughly compound them all.
This charm, once set and left to stand,
Will cast a blight on any land.

Barbara Roe

1961

How Say You?

(Evidence in a divorce case is reported to have included a photograph of a man and woman lying unclothed on a sofa. Competitors were invited to consider themselves as one of the couple and to provide an explanation of the innocence of the situation)

Look, he says, if it embarrasses you that much to play the Maja, I'll set the shutter to go off in three minutes time, then you get set and it'll photograph you automatically while I'm outside. So I stripped and got on the sofa while he fixed it all up, but just as he was going outside I said Will this do? and he said Christ no, you're lying like a sack of potatoes. It's because your sofa's so damned narrow, I said. Narrow? he shouts, there'd be room for two of us on the bloody thing! and gets on to prove it. All right all right, I said, anyway it makes me all coy being naked, wouldn't you be? The hell I would, he says, pulling off his shirt, just watch me! and he strips too. He's a bit like that. Then the camera went off.

Stephen Sedley

— Are you aware that you appear unclothed in this photograph?
— I am.
— What kind of photograph is it?
— It is an infra-red photograph.
— Why do you appear unclothed?
— We are wearing polarised polyacrylesterene fibre.
— And polarised polyacrylesterene does not show in infra-red photographs?
— That is correct.
— How do you come to be lying on this sofa?
— Counsel is holding the photograph the wrong way up. We are not lying on the sofa. We are carrying it out of the room.

Miles Burrows

The Sword of Stalingrad

(*Evelyn Waugh's* Unconditional Surrender *mentions a wartime literary competition which called for an* 'Ode to the Sword of Stalingrad'. *In the light of the destalinisation of the USSR, odes suitable to 1961 were requested*)

The Sword of Stalingrad was earned
By people tough as steel
Who, even as their city burned,
Made Hitler's armies reel.
And Winston Churchill, at Tehran,
Passed the sword over to That Man
Whose name (in view of Krushchev's ban)
It's safer to conceal.
The Sword of Stalingrad hangs now
In Volgograd instead;
And locals, fearful of a row,
Leave the old name unsaid,
Because the Kremlin's present crew,
By writing history anew,
Did what the Germans couldn't do –
Killed Stalingrad stone dead.

Peter Veale

Debated blade, what good intent
Has led to red embarrassment!
Given a name which, wrought with fire and blood,
Appears now to the Party to be mud!
The Man of Steel, who erred,
Is re-interred,
To lie unhonoured earth beneath;
Will they now hide you in some shabby sheath –
He to be common dust
And you allowed to rust,
Or, with a different name, mayhap,
Will you commemorate some other chap?
Ah, better not!

Who can foretell the lot
Of any idol pedestalled today?
Will you be tops tomorrow, still, Oh K?

W. K. Holmes

Excellent Openings

(A conversation between a Sixth Former and his Careers Master. The first entry here will confirm unsuccessful competitors' worst fears)

CM. You want a soft job, with a small but regular income? Why not Competition-setting?

SF. What do you have to do for that?

CM. Quite simple! You take a topical subject out of the newspaper, make up a list of well-known writers, and combine them.
>For example: 'Give an imaginary extract from the works of Shakespeare, Johnson, P. G. Wodehouse, Homer, Kingsley Amis, or Browning, on the Common Market.'

SF. But isn't it an awful swot, reading all the entries? And how do I judge them, if I haven't read all those blasted authors?

CM. Oh well, there are half a dozen regular prize-winners (I can give you their names). Pick out their entries, and select two or three of them in rotation; add a few others at random, and shy the rest into the basket! The thing's a lottery, anyway!

R. Kennard Davis

SF. Advise me, sir.

CM. H'm. Poor intellectual capacity, offset by considerable cunning; moral integrity nil; dull, seemingly respectable features ... Crampe, if you were there already, I would say Archbishop, Prime Minister or King, but you would never top the lower slopes. How about blackmail?

SF. Sir?

CM. Public School porter.

SF. That's not much of a job, sir.

CM. Crampe, nobody pays attention to a background official. Be efficient. Keep your eyes and ears open, that's all. Study the scribbles in the school bogs, watch who does them, take photographs. Look in the desks for obscene post-cards. See what the masters are up to with boys they keep in late. That sort of thing. Tape recorder. Concealed microphones. Lots of famous people have sons at a public school, Crampe, people with money, people who'd pay, people who daren't be touched by scandal. The Governors don't like scandal either. Savvy?

J. A. Lindon

My Old Man's A Dustman

(*A* Panorama *programme revealed the existence of a pre-11-plus cramming school, geared to the production of members of the Meritocracy. Competitors provided essays from three of the pupils on 'What I Want To Be When I Grow Up'*)

I want to be like dad he kin lift to two bins at a time an bring home useful things like a hardly borke crikit bat and beet Mister jensen on duble twenny but mum she says I got to go that ther skule an mak muney and cud be state ajent or perfesser an woh dus that missis migwire think she is putin on airs becos of jenifer passing. and wonce a kertin mum use it was ony tore a litle and anyway I dont thik think he hardly smels at al and thats I want to be.

Henry Walter

I want to be a Working Class because they get everything these days. My dad is onely a ratpayer and he has to keep up curtain Stundards like school uniforms etc. but the Working Classes are aloud to speak Badly and get free TV and subsided housing and 20 pounds per week with no Responcebility and dress all anyhow because they go to commony schools. Ratpairs subsides all these HP amenities. Working Classes doe not have to live in Residential

Areas, they can play in the street. My dad says i must be a pre-fissional man or else a Tikeover or else go to Rotesia where there is more scope for Intinative. But I dont knoe so much.

Trooper Jones

When I grow up I would like to be a Stattus' simbol.

A stattus' Simbol is a important man even better than our niebour mister Jones': althought dad said therd be a photoe-finish. Being a Stattus' Simbol is not easy according to dad, and requires consider-able tenacety – like when I avoidid takeing the 11+ for monthes with constant absences' and letters from mums sychatrist and that.

Dad sold the car, it was really a Comercial vehicle but dad said always reffer to it as the car so we could go to the cramming school! Since; my edukcation has progressed by leaps & bounds.

A stattus' simbol is expeckted to ware a colar & tie but I am not detered.

Ken Geering

Not Yeti

(*Requiems in verse for the Yeti*)

For many years, say nigh on eighty,
We searched and searched to find you, Yeti;
Tried ways honest, tried ways cheaty
To trail and trap elusive Yeti.
Spoke to those who said they'd met 'e,
All was illusion, thin-air Yeti.
No more shall stirring headline greet I;
Farewell, my non-existent Yeti.

L. G. Udall

Oh, you that never were,
But are what we shall be
When certain things occur

Which all of us foresee!
At least you had a name,
Your witnesses and fame!

Who rashly will declare
Of us, in years ahead,
'They lived!', or greatly care
For truths about the dead?

Your non-existent feet
Left traces in the snow
Which were discussed with heat
By people in the know.
Will anyone discuss
Such traces left by us?

A. M. Sayers

Make It Oundle For Oswald

*(The time may yet come when the public schools will have to advertise.
Competitors anticipated this event in the style of various newspapers,
and one famous house-agent)*

TOP PEOPLE GO TO TOP SCHOOLS
But only the TOP top school is good enough for your boy.

Shelley and James Fisher, Gladstone and Humphrey Lyttelton –
    what have these Top Ones in common?
They're all Old Etonians.
Remember this, when considering scholastic summitry for *your* boy.
Uniquely combining traditional and modern ('Top' and 'Pop'),
    Eton bestows on its alumni a lifetime's innate consciousness
    of effortless superiority.
Do you think of Eton simply as a 'Distant prospect' (yes, we had
    Gray, too) because you're crippled by Surtax?
    Write for free brochure describing our Easy Terms.
(The Times)

Stanley J. Sharpless

TWILIGHT CONTENTMENT

A day's work completed. Important deals arranged, influential contacts established, labour force pacified. A delightful dinner. Now for a glass of port and . . . *a book*. To relive the excitements of the Gallic Wars or savour once again the raucous delights of Restoration Theatre? Perhaps . . .

This is the fourth of a series of ten advertisements issued by the Governors of Eton College in the interests of the cultural life of the nation.

(*Daily Telegraph*)

P. Natal

REPTON

To unsuccessful applicants who missed recent L.m.e.h. Palace vacancy, I can offer a few places for 11-plus failures in EPISCOPAL KINDERGARTEN within spitting distance of Burton-upon-Trent. The rambling Victorian buildings are somewhat dilapidated since the boys said goodbye to Mr CHIPS, but virginia creeper covers the cracks. If there were any baths, I *didn't* see them. Teaching quite decent and administration first-class. Recommended to class-conscious clause-4 abolitionists and Tory matrons campaigning for corporal punishment, cold showers, the Empire and tapioca pudding. IMMEDIATE ENTRY to donors of *substantial* cheques to School's quater-centenary fund. – Rex Rivers

(*Observer*)

A. D. Bennett Jones

No Moaning At The Bar

(*A comment, in the poet's own style, on the fact that Farringford House, Tennyson's old home in the Isle of Wight, is now a hotel*)

Where the Laureate on his laurels
    Rested in a bygone day,
Persons who have never read him,

94

If they can afford it, stay.
His is not the first of dwellings
    Where the great their ease have spent
Serving now commercial uses –
    Precedent to precedent.
Does at dusk some startled tourist
    Ask another, *What is that*?
Glimpsing a forbidding shadow
    In a sombre cloak and hat?
Through the unremitting radio
    Does at times a querulous croak
Voice a comment on the racket
    From a long-lived Talking Oak?
If he lingers round in spirit,
    Does he thank his lucky stars
That he lived ere his approaches
    Were a parking-place for cars?
Yet perhaps he would have noted,
    In his best descriptive strain,
How the jammed array resembled
    Bright-shelled beetles in the rain.
May there be, amongst the many,
    One who eats his eggs and ham,
Quaffs his morning tea or cocktail,
    Murmuring 'In Memoriam!'

W. K. Holmes

Irish Television

(*With the beginning of Irish TV, some difficulty was anticipated in collecting the licence fee as Irish viewers could already watch British TV for nothing. An Irish reaction to this situation was asked for*)

JAMES JOYCE

Irish dancing I suppose a lot of flatchested little girls jigging up and down with their medals rattling hed pay up of course glued to

95

the set night after night to see could he catch a glimpse of something he shouldnt ah but the other now with those lovely announcers so clean whats the word cleanlimbed and their beautiful English voices apologising with every breath for having spoken at all as if theyd just peed on the carpet now that d be worth it but sure thats free anyway I wonder now could we hide the aerial some way.

Ian Sainsbury

Oh I See

(*The Facts of Life explained by Lord Montgomery*)

All normal young people want to do this thing. It is natural, like fighting.

As in my battles with Rommel, there should be mutual respect. Then it can be quite a good party.

The object of the exercise should be reproduction. I certainly found this was the case in China, a country which greatly impressed me.

I think it is better if people doing this thing do not drink or smoke. That, of course, is a purely personal view.

Peter Veale

You Loved
the Film Now Read the Book

(*Blurbs for various publications hitherto neglected in the field of advertisement*)

GEORGICS IV

A thin scream cuts through the silence of the lonely hills and a dark figure, maddened with primitive passion, stumbles back to his bee-hives, running from the lovely girl he hounded to death . . .

96

In rapid, taut strokes, P. V. Maro lays bare the soul of a nympholept – Aristaeus, the Libyan teenager whose shadow seared the soul of the woman he loved and the strange musician who mourned her.

This haunting study of a man accursed overflows with a fabulous selection of *outré* characters – Proteus, the weird old beachcomber. Cyrene, the girl who followed the sun. Orpheus, gentle victim of ruthless women . . .

The rumbustious (yet compassionate) narrative concludes on a new note of hope and a virile, un-modish patriotism which augurs well for Maro's forthcoming epic of love and war in Italy and North Africa.

Trooper Jones

THE OLD TESTAMENT

Grizzled, patriarchal God, owner of enormous Paradise Ranch, settles two homesteaders, Adam and Eve, on his spread to see how they prosper. All goes well till wily B. L. Zeebub, an untrustworthy ranch hand fired by God, stirs the newcomers to trouble and God forces them off his rich rangeland into swampy country. *The Old Testament* traces the struggle of Adam and Eve's offspring to regain the good, green pasture of Paradise Ranch. This action-filled tale is told in easy, rambling prose, full of the sound and smell of frontier days in Old Palestine.

Charles Monaghan

1962

Wearing White for Bredon United

(*The scholarship of Mr John Sparrow has unearthed a pattern of sexual deviation in* Lady Chatterley's Lover. *Competitors cheerfully dug for new meanings in other works, hitherto sacrosanct*)

A SHROPSHIRE LAD

It is a pity that criticism has hitherto confined itself to the more frivolous aspects of this poem – the inversion, narcissism, military fetishism, noose nostalgia, necrophily, solipsism, and a hundred other commonplaces of the analyst's couch. Concern with such trivia has obscured the true drift of the sequence. It is, of course, a thinly-disguised plea for the extension of mid-week soccer.

In XVII, Housman recalls yearningly how,

> Twice a week the winter through
> Here stood I to keep the goal.

'Twice a week', you notice: not 'once' as in *our* decadent day. In XXVII, he asks:

> Is football playing
> Along the river shore?

at the same time as he enquires:

> Is my team ploughing?

No one ploughs on Saturday afternoon. The reference is, then, clearly to a *mid-week* fixture. The case is clinched however by two oft-derided lines:

> The goal stands up, the keeper
> Stands up to keep the goal.

Is this just a ludicrous imitation of a famous Horatian mannerism? Of course not. The reiteration is functional, counselling a hebdomadal reiteration of the process, namely the *game*. Other, rather more esoteric pointers abound . . .

Martin Fagg

My Husband and I

(A nonsense poem in the manner of Edward Lear and with a present-day flavour)

They went on a Cottonwool Tour, they did,
    On a Cottonwool Tour for two!
With a scrupulous nurse and a maundy purse
And a reegle-me-ree and a Dumble-bee
And an Ooofah-fox in a washable box
    And a bottle of crawfy Goo.

And all the Cottonwool people say:
'Oh runcible couple! Hooray! Hooray!
They make us Dames and they teach us Games
    And they wave and smile all day!
For they come from the land of the Dimble-folk,
Good-gracious lady and popular bloke,
They open the fête and present the prize,
Oh, we never will sunder our Cottonwool ties!'

So they gave them a silver snorkel
And a parachute made of clay
And a sporty bonnet of Corgi tails
    To save for a rainy day,
As the sun set low on the Oompah
    And they sadly sailed away.

Trooper Jones

Time!

(When Sonny Liston became heavyweight champion of the world, it was thought that the American press might have to rescue him from his seamy past and produce a bright new image for national perusal. Competitors were asked to produce passages from Time *magazine on these lines)*

One-time delinquent Charles (Sonny) Liston fingered a neck-slung crucifix after blasting faltering Floyd (What-hit-me?) Patterson.

Confided Sonny: 'It's Him up there I got to thank. I know the great American public will give me the same break He's given me.'

Humbly proffered for *Time*'s respectful inspection was the fabulous fist with which Sonny had socked his way to fame and fortune. Tenderly clutched in the other, a battered Bible from which once-underprivileged Liston is learning to read.

Promised Prodigal Sonny: 'Yep, now I'm champ beating old dames for pennies is definitely out.' We believe him.

Keith Dimmer

Gigantic, fun-loving, extroverted T.C. (for Top Cat) Liston ducked powerful, well co-ordinated frame through ropes and joined two religious, surpliced priests devoutly drinking coffee in corner of plushy, uptown gym. Quipped formerly much misunderstood practical joker Sonny (real name Charles) 'I'm a peace-loving guy at heart' and, throwing gentle left hook at reverend jaw, ad libbed 'State Pen. sure is mightier than the sword.' Later, at a quiet, touching ceremony attended only by world's presscorps élite, Champion Liston gifted solid, leather-covered punch-bag to club for underprivileged boys. Insisted he, movingly and with catch voicewise 'Clubs like this might have saved my old friends Blinky Palermo, Frankie Carbo and Johnny Vitale getting where they are today.' Silently, humbly, a World Champion remembered his less fortunate, erstwhile companions. Outsized in heart as all else is Charles Liston.

R. A. K. Wright

Hic Jacet

(Premature verse epitaph for a present-day public figure)

JOHN GORDON

Believing that his hate for queers
    Proclaimed his love for God,
He now (of all queer things, my dears)
    Lies under his first sod.

Paul Dehn

Consumer Guides

(Reports in the manner of Which? *At this time, politicians were just recovering from the Macmillan massacre)*

THE CABINET

We were about to begin the British Standard tests on the full range of CABINET utensils when no fewer than a third were precipitately withdrawn by the manufacturer. We must say that we find the sudden suspension of these much-publicized lines difficult to reconcile with the manufacturer's simultaneous announcement of complete faith in the efficiency of their performance. We understand that, in *fact*, the company had decided that the KIL-MUIR model was obsolete, the LLOYD insufficiently flexible and the ECCLES altogether too shoddy and gimcrack. The withdrawal of HILL was, we gather, due to widely-felt misgivings over the brain-weight ratio. The company has added to public confusion by renaming several of the brands retained. The BUTLER, for instance, has been subjected to yet another change of description; for all of which, it remains exactly the same wan and utterly unexciting product.

Martin Fagg

RELIGIOUS DENOMINATIONS

This investigation was very expensive emotionally, and we are grateful to 153 members of CA who undertook user-trials of the four denominations surveyed. All four are nationally distributed, though there may be occasional local difficulty in obtaining supply. They were tested for ease and convenience of belief, social status and spread, financial sacrifice expected and aesthetic appeal. Unfortunately, we were unable to evolve a reliable measurement of holiness, but we believe this omission does not unduly affect the value of the inquiry.

Roman Catholic: Comprehensive socially, and artistic users liked its liturgy. But low credibility, and most married believers will find its demands excessive.

Methodist: Few disciples in AB groups. One model tested over-stressed joys of heaven, and turned out not to be properly earthed.

Baptist: This brand unprecedentedly insisted on subjecting the consumer to an immersion test. Not recommended.

Anglican: Some complaints from angry young men, but most members will find a model to fit their requirements. Socially acceptable and cheap to run. Best buy.

Christopher Prout

But Lord! To See
The Absurd Nature of Englishmen

(*Part of Pepys' diary for three days during 1957–1961*)

Friday: Though it is but a foolery to watch it much, did observe on Television an argument between partisans of either faction on the state of the body politic. Thought that the realm is soon like to be in a most mischievous taking, should its affairs be long entrusted to such a parcel of fellows.

Saturday: Abroad in the evening to Soho where there be yet a varied abundance of gamesome wenches, to judge from the cards that do give advertisement of them from the windows; yet now all the time withindoors, which does make for a notable increase of decency. My wife, poor wretch!, very querulous on my return.

Sunday: Up betimes, to pray for my sins; and later to St Pauls though the way was foul. The way of this world like to be fouler still, says Dr Collins, a mighty warm preacher, in his sermon. Cast down by this, but took a fine nap and woke much refreshed. And so home to a baron of beef – a great consolation to the flesh.

Martin Fagg

Sept. 16th: To the Theatre to see *Beyond the Fringe*, where a sermon pleased me mightily, being comicall. One ripped up PM and stirred all to merriment with talk on armpits. But all were loyall and stood for 'Queen'.

Sept. 17th (Lord's Day). In rain to Trafalgar Squarc to see rebels defying Police by sitting downe. I told friendly Whitehall man I would hang them all and he telling me to return later when I might see good sport. But on way home did meet Mrs Rebecca, now in Strip-Tease business and she did give me free ticket.

Sept. 18th: In *Times* this morning read of dangers of 'fall-out' and feared expense of shelter, but My Lord called telling me that deep shelter for Queen and us, all prepared. God be thanked.

P. W. R. Foot

Circulation-Builders

(*In 1962, the sober* Observer *stooped to a special feature on the hunt for the Loch Ness monster. Competitors supplied other sober features aimed at boosting circulation*)

Next week the *Observer* publishes the result of a special inquiry into an undramatic but nonetheless vital aspect of librarianship: the judicious elimination of unwanted books. Pressure on shelf space in many of Britain's municipal libraries has reached crisis point. A rational approach to the problem of obsolescence has become urgent.

But what principles – if, indeed, any – are being followed? PHILIP TOYNBEE has spent three weeks studying the methods of 18 representative libraries. In several, he found, any book that has not been borrowed for a year is rejected outright. Is this fair to the author in a dark green binding on a bottom shelf? Another library first puts such doubtful books in a weekly display, 'We Liked These'. Should this practice be generally adopted? Watch next week for Toynbee's unflinchingly thorough report and his controversial conclusions.

John Wardroper

The *Oberver* has secured exclusive rights in the epic story of the Channel Tunnel. Every Sunday for the five years the tunnel takes to build, a brilliant *Observer* team will bring you a foot-by-foot account of progress through the Channel's oozy bed. Tynan will be there to report the biggest engineering drama of all time. Jennings will relay oddities and humour from the depths. Toynbee will consider the sexual symbolism of tunnelling in literature, while Katherine Whitehorn keeps a sharp eye on tunnel fashions. The extra revenue from increased sales will go to the creation of an *Observer* Trust Fund for the advancement of tunnel and sewer technology in the undeveloped countries. If a bridge is decided on instead of a tunnel, it will, of course, be fully covered by our Bridge Correspondent.

Stanley J. Sharpless

1963

Tread Thou In Them Boldly

(Lord Mansfield, a Tory peer and, in 1962, Lord High Commissioner to the Church of Scotland, suggested that he would like to see 'the treadmill introduced once more'. Competitors provided a Daily Express *leader on the subject, together with a Home Office Circular)*

DAILY EXPRESS

At last.

Someone has spoken out. Someone with courage.

A peer of the realm, who is both a patriot and a churchman, has suggested that the vast army of thugs and layabouts that you, the taxpayer, maintain at vast expense in Her Majesty's prisons, should actually earn their bread by the sweat of their brow.

The treadmill was an indispensable feature of our prisons in the days when this nation was climbing to greatness.

Today it has disappeared.

And today we are being kicked around and insulted by twopenny-halfpenny little tinpot states that in the old days we could have thrashed singlehanded before breakfast.

There is a moral here somewhere.

Lord Mansfield's family have already rendered important services to the nation. This suggestion is not the least among them.

For 'the evil-doer shall tread the path of affliction.'

It is written.

So be it.

Martin Fagg

HOME OFFICE CIRCULAR

Attention is drawn to the fact that all Corrective Training Wheels are supplied with either a right-hand or a left-hand drive. Medical experts have proved that considerable unnecessary suffering may be inflicted on prisoners forced to use a wheel for which they are not properly orientated. All prisoners must therefore undergo Orientation Tests as laid down in Home Office leaflet BX 1896 (Price 2d.), and the result placed upon the prisoner's record card and the prisoner, with the appropriate branding-iron. Brands of the letter 'L' or 'R' in Times Roman caps (not exceeding 24 point for males, and 18 point for females) should be placed not less than 2 inches below the right elbow on the forearm. Where no right forearm is available, consultation should be made to Home Office leaflet ZV 6754A 'Extra Approved Branding Places' (Price 1d.).

E. O. Parrott

Rhyming Alphabet

(*Alphabets were requested on any contemporary (1963) political event*)

A   was an Agent, suborning a spy.
B   was the Blackmail he chose to apply.
C   was a Clerk who was secretly queer.
D,   the Disclosures extorted through fear.
E,   the Exposure that clerk could not bear.
F   for our Freedoms which pooves do not share.
G   for our Gaols, housing inverts and spies.
H   for our Hacks who amuse us with lies.
I,   their 'Inquiries' – char, bar and invention.
J   for our Jokes, too improper to mention.
K   for our Kink – we think *everyone*'s queer.
L   was a Letter beginning 'My dear . . .'.
M   was a Minister, slandered and sacked.
N   is for Nonsense presented as fact.
O,   Oleaginous hatchet-man Brown.
P,   a PM who lets everyone down.
Q   is for Question-time, slimy with smears.
R,   the Replies, rightly greeted with jeers.
S   is for 'Socialists' spreading the muck.
T   is for Tories with no bloody pluck.

U   is our Upright and ethical Press.
V, Vows of silence *re* source – or *re* guess.
W, Ways of improving security.
X, the new X-Ray for probing impurity.
Y's *you* – and me – with our jailing and spying.
Z   is this Zoo where we're living – or dying.

Trooper Jones

Baron Munchausen

(The astounding adventures of Baron Munchausen were mediated to the world by Rudolph Raspe as long ago as 1785. Anecdotes were requested from their 1963 sequel)

I was mildly surprised when Mr Macmillan, choking violently on an indulgent draught of cocoa, coughed, and lost his head from his shoulders. I retrieved it from the carpet and set it back upon his neck. As I did so, I saw, through the aperture in his torso, an intricate system of flashing transistors. Immediately sensible of the unspoken question in my eyes, he addressed this confidence to me. That the real Macmillan had many years previously been grossly injured in a hunting accident. A startled grouse had taken wing in his direction with such velocity that it entered his gaping mouth, pierced his palate, and flew into his brain. There it fluttered around his head, hunger directing its only available diet. For the gravest political reasons, this misadventure was not made public. A Mr Tussaud constructed a marvellous replica, which was operated through an elaborate console in Washington. Government by short wave ensures consistency, coordination and central control. In these troubled times, there is much to commend it.

Russell Lucas

In the Britannic Islands I found despair at failure to launch a vehicle into heavenly space; so I caused to be constructed an aerial ship pierced at its base, like a colander, into 60 large holes. Printers and pastry-cooks furnished rice-paper sheets, bearing upon them the printed promises of all political parties; these were fed to 60 citizens who entered the ship and sat down, each upon a hole. So void of content was the sustenance that the bowels of these gallant men were invaded by a mighty flatulence which promptly escaped through three-score breech-plugged holes. To a sound like a fanfare of my Emperor's trumpeters, the ship rose from its platform and, gathering speed, disappeared into the heavens. Many feared that their brave compatriots might not return but I reminded them of what an Englishman can always achieve on his second wind.

Lyndon Irving

Jubilation

(*A poem, in the manner of William McGonagall, on the New Statesman's 50th Jubilee*)

'Twas in the year 1913 that you first the daylight saw,
Which is an interesting date to remember being exactly one year
    before the outbreak of the First World War;
And almost every week since then you duly have appeared,
And many are the abuses that by thy words have been seared.
And still every week you emerge your enemies to rile,
From the premises known to one and all as 10 Great Turnstile.
Indeed, in the good old days, it was said, unless report be a fibber,
That your perusers did often fall down, foam at the mouth and
    gibber.
Your editor was for many years one Kingsley Martin,
And it was work that assuredly he had his innermost heart in;
And it did one good to think of him sitting up there in his eyrie,
Scribbling away day and night at the pages of his 'London Diary'.
And the present editor is Mr John Freeman,
Whom I have no hesitation to deem an
Upright and most worthy man, known to us all from *Face to Face*,
Where most of his questions do give his subjects a most hearty
    grimace.
And there are also film, play, art and music critics writing us to
    please,

Who must spend their time rushing about London as busy as
 bumble bees.
And then there is 'This England', which records what many good
 folk have thought,
And my only complaint is that there is no 'This Scotland', as
 indeed there ought . . .

Martin Fagg

Marion's Nose Looks Red and Raw

(A modern version of Shakespeare's 'When icicles hang by the wall')

When icicles encrust the bath,
    And wheels churn madly in the snow,
And glaciers line the garden path,
    And everywhere's too far to go.
When lights go out, and gas runs short,
Then daily do the Boards exhort:
'Switch off, conserve, economize!'
For winter takes them by surprise.

When plumbers' boots thud through the hall,
    And frozen privies close the schools,
And trains bog down and buses crawl,
    And Drake and Lawton guess the Pools,
When coal is low and taps run dry,
The Boards repeat their plaintive cry:
'Switch off, economize, conserve!'
May God forgive their bloody nerve!

Peter Veale

Extremely Untired of London

(The Yale editors of the Boswell papers continue their indefatigable labours. The latest volume contained fresh material on Johnson. Competitors were invited to submit extracts from a future instalment showing the Doctor in a new and wholly unexpected light)

Returning from our weekly visit to the Stews, the Doctor was in excellent humour. I was in a deep melancholy, usual on such occasions, and hummed a tune to raise my spirits. *Johnson*: 'That was a very pretty *Lay*.' *Boswell*: 'Some little thing from Ossian, I believe.' *Johnson*: 'Spoken like a true Scot. I had not even considered the provenance of the lady.' Whereupon I saw he was in one of his *carnal* moods. *Johnson*: 'I noticed ————' (naming a prominent Whig) 'slipping out of the chamber as I entered. Necessity makes strange bedfellows.' *Boswell*: 'It is a Necessity of which I am ashamed.' *Johnson*: 'Who are we to question the ordinances of the Almighty? Doubtless God could have devised other ways of propagating the species. Praise be that He did not choose to do so. We are uxorious and philoprogenitive by divine decree; to gainsay it were a kind of blasphemy. Truly the bed is a great *Leveller*. The prophet, the poet and the prostitute are all equal in bed. Sir, I would rate the inventor of the bed alongside the inventor of the wheel.' He nudged me with his elbow. 'Only six more days, Bozzie; six more days.'

Stanley J. Sharpless

Going at midday to Dr Johnson's chambers in the Inner Temple, I was astonished to find him seated on a hard chair in the middle of the room, with his hose, buckled shoes and breeches removed, and his feet in a pan of steaming water.

'Sir, are you ill?' I inquired anxiously.

'No, sir. I am in rude health, I am glad to say. I have been exercising my nether limbs, in order to increase their muscular potentialities.'

'What, sir! would you frolic, would you learn dancing?'

'No, sir. It is my intention to become a runner. I have a race on hand. That insolent footman of Lord Chesterfield's dared to mock at my uncouth gait, but I'll show him, sir, I'll show him.'

'He is reputed to be very fleet.'

'Why, Mr Boswell, if that be so, then it must be the hare and the tortoise over again.'

'Sir, will you grease your legs?'

'Why, sir, for a purse of two hundred sovereigns they may butter my hams or what they will, an I reach Aldgate first. Sir, he called me a lurching leviathan, but I'll show him my heels.'

R. A. McKenzie

No Newdigate

(The Newdigate prize for English verse was not awarded at Oxford in 1963 as the entries were too few and feeble. Budding NS poets were asked to comment on this in a poem likely to recommend itself to the taste of a rather old-fashioned academic adjudicator)

Sweet Isis sighs, her verdant banks between,
To view the grimly changed Oxonian scene
Where erst the thronging poets lov'd to bring
Their brain-bred firstlings in proud offering,
The best their midnight musings might devise
To gain acclaim and win the laurelled prize.
Alas! that modern thought has thrust aside
The Muse to languish in forgotten pride,
For now our Youth esteems it greater pleasure
To *tread* – not seek, to grace his theme – a measure,
Nor loves the Cup of Poesy to fill
With honey'd pourings from Hymettus' Hill;
Ah, not today unto those steadfast towers
Comes Inspiration from her Attic bowers.
The mists of Time obscure Parnassus' height,
Chill winds of Change obstruct the Muses' flight.

Nancy Gunter

1964

Intimations of Immorality

(*Competitors were invited to complete, in their own way, Wordsworth's poem:*

> *Strange fits of passion have I known:*
> *And I will dare to tell,*
> *But in the Lover's ear alone,*
> *What once to me befell.*)

I wound my watch one winter night
And, yawning, made for bed
When on the pillow snowy white,
I saw a young maid's head.

Her eyes seemed heavy closed in sleep,
Her hair a mass of curls;
I thought she looked more like a sheep
Than many Lakeland girls.

Then conscious of the night air chill,
I felt my legs a-quiver.
'To Hell', I thought, 'with daffodil
And primrose by the river.'

My passion rose (with every sign)
And nought could hold me back.
With flat of hand, that form supine
I gave a gentle smack.

But horror! In that chamber dark
I struck no Dian's belly.
Then 'Bad luck, Bill – another lark!'
Spoke out the voice of Shelley.

Strange fits of passion have I known
Between my bedroom sheets.
What I'd have done I dare not own
If Shelly'd been John Keats.

Lyndon Irving

Penny Plain
and Ninepence Coloured

(*Colour-supplements are becoming the order of the newspaper day or week. Competitors were asked to describe the colour-supplement of any publication so far free from colour*)

CHURCH TIMES

After the magnificent Hieronimus Bosch cover picture, with the bold question 'Do We Still Believe in This?', the Bishop of Woolwich's enlightened article on Hell was something of an anti-climax. However, there was much to praise in this first issue. I enjoyed the intimate pictures of the Archbishop of Canterbury at home, with verses specially written by John Betjeman ('Large in the rose garden looms Dr Ramsey, Patriarch, leader and chum to us all'). Nicolas Stacey's pen portraits of 'hip' clerics were nicely done, though some of the photographs of vestry rhythm-and-blues groups may have offended older readers. Here and there the influence of popular newspapers was startlingly evident, as in the feature 'Vestment Trends' ('The Rev. Passmore Simcox sets the pace with grace in this get-up-and-go saffron surplice...'). I was also a little surprised to see an item called 'Where Are They Now?', dealing with clergy unfrocked by the consistory courts over the past half-century. On the whole, though, dignity and taste were maintained and nowhere better than in Mr Raymond Postgate's excellent and beautifully illustrated article on New Ideas in Communion Wine.

Peter Veale

Back by Christmas

(On the occasion of the 50th anniversary of the outbreak of World War I, a poem was asked for, entitled 'August, 1914')

My father had the telegram when I
Could barely read. An autumn victory,
The voices sang, embarked at midnight: then
Silence, massively emptied of its men.
Black ribs of newsprint bulked across the page.
Night fears kept me awake; it was my age,
But whispers too, and once an earthquake noise
Smelling of cordite after. Closed to boys
The foreshore, stalked by sentries. A cap came
Bobbing the waves; a German name
Rewarded trespass. So began the tide
Of questions no one answered. Summer died
Into a labyrinth without guiding rope,
Good times mislaid, groping through adult hope,
I held my childhood on a four-year lease
Till in red chalk the pavements shouted Peace.

Robert Gittings

Dear Diary

(The usual prizes were offered for the most surprising extract from a pre-1900 diary hitherto unpublished)

OSCAR WILDE, 1894

Monday: Again I reflect, how boring life is! My hard, gem-like flame flickers and dies when, as was the case this morning, I felt impelled to resume work on this tedious play, *Earnest*. The ultimate *raison d'être* of Art is Eat – no, I can't use that. I really must arrange one of my secret meetings with Rudyard – such a friend, really. But if only my Yellow Book friends knew the source of most of my material!

Tuesday: At lunch today with Bosie. The cod and chips were very good. We laughed over gin at the origin of his nickname (Boozie, as all must know) and I got vinegar on my cravat. Never mind. We talked again of opening a small chain of tobacconists if *Earnest* goes well. I asked him if he knew any suitable jokes that I could use. He said no.

Wednesday: Saw Frank Harris in the Strand this morning. I utterly admired that man until last year he took me aside and made me the confessor of his virginity. Still, I felt enough camaraderie towards him to confide my growing attraction towards the Methodist Church. Shall I go over in the end, I wonder?

Thursday: At tea with Bosie and quite shocked and disgusted! Told me Harris made a suggestion quite repellent to him – no details here. To blot out this episode, we got rather merry and finding ourselves near Hyde Park, took two ladies we met there to a small hotel in Bayswater.

Friday: A sore head this morning. Wonder if Shaw would collaborate in something? Fatigued with *Earnest*, walked along Fleet Street and met Carson standing outside urinal. Asked him if *he* knew any good jokes for *Earnest*.

Peter Rowlett

Pardon!

(*Among subjects for occasional poems listed by William Shenstone, the 18th-century writer, was: To his mistress on her declaring that she loved parsnips better than potatoes*)

Madam, when first I came to woo
I proffered onions, cabbage too;
But finally I urged you bedwards
With half a pound of nice King Edwards.

Alas! Your fickle taste has turned,
The humble Murphy now is spurned;
Some sneaking rival, in base fashion,
With parsnips has engaged your passion.

Dishonoured now your solemn pledge
That only I should choose your veg;
Forgotten, too, those pretty blushes
When first I called you my Pomme Duchesse.

Potatoes, I have always found,
Are simple, honest, bluff and sound;
The parsnip's windy, mean and caddish,
Bastard of carrot and horseradish.

I ask you, Madam, what is worse
Than flatulence, the parsnip's curse?
The world agrees a lady's poise is
Sadly impaired by parsnip noises.

Peter Veale

We Regret To Announce

(*Competitors provided, on behalf of the authors concerned, the 'last moments' of some famous characters in literature*)

MR SALTEENA

Dam and blarst said Mr Salteena flinging aside his wifes prayer book I shall go and see Ethel today. He cheerd up and put on his suit of velvit cote and green knickerbockers. He carefully rubbd the seat part with oderclone witch had gone shiny from horse galloping. He poked the doorbell of Ethels manshon with his riding crop. If this is sin I like it thought Mr Salteena. A maid showed him into a costly room with gay sofas. He helped himself to a large wiskey and took a fat sigar. A lovely vishon came it was Ethel. Mr Salteena sprang to his feet and said egerly I cannot stand sour grapes and ashes any longer come away with me. You filty beast gasped Ethel the wages of Sin is Deth. She took a little gun from a fringy evenig bag and shot him. Mr Salteena died.

P. M. Robertson

MR MICAWBER

I am very sensible of the peregrinations and vicissitudes through which I have travelled and passed since I left the mother country for the Southern continent. I have risen to lofty altitudes after sinking to abysmal depths – in short, I have had my ups and downs. My fellow citizens of Port Middlebay once expressed the wish that I might never leave them except to better myself and now the time has arrived when their hope is fulfilled. I am gratified that all my olive branches have grown to sturdy trees and, surrounding the dear wife of my bosom, Mrs Micawber, are gathered here to tender their threnodic valedictions to me, and their filial devotion to her, as I leave for the bourne from which no traveller returns – in short, Heaven. Because I have languished incarcerated in a debtors' prison I have striven, as a magistrate, to render to every man his due – in short, to be just – and I trust that my whilom pecuniary subterfuges may be forgiven as I have endeavoured to extricate others from their financial embarrassment. And now that my terrestrial sojourn is drawing to its conclusion I am waiting for nothing to turn up – except my toes.

Vera Telfer

White Mischief

(The least conventional incident from an autobiography by Evelyn Waugh)

The conversion of the Bazubi tribe who inhabit, and proliferate along, the East African littoral was one of my least publicised spiritual triumphs. To lead them from Islam to the Vatican was attended with many difficulties, not the least of which was to persuade them that German philologists had long ago accepted that a complicated series of vowel and consonantal shifts proved Mahomed to be the same name as Jesus. There remained after this the black brothers' extraordinary addiction to non-alcoholic beverages such as human haemoglobin in its natural aqueous suspension: this struck at the very roots of my efforts to explain transubstantiation. We experimented, in the early trial masses, with a mixture of blood and Coca-Cola and when this was accepted we reduced the blood content until at last pure 'Coke' was employed. To the African palate this drink was so repulsive that the addition of a little Chambertin was regarded as a marked improvement and, *poco a poco*, I finally weaned my unpleasant friends from blood to *vino puro*. The day this was achieved the whole tribe went down with enteritis and I was forced to take my leave.

Lyndon Irving ·

More Cautionary Tales

(*Of, again, the up-to-date kind*)

At sixteen Jayne was at her Best,
With Smiling Buttocks, Beaming Breast,
A modern Girl, right in the Swing,
Who'd scream at Almost Anything.
The Group that served her Cultural Needs
Was called the Swinging Centipedes.
Jayne loved the Lead Guitarist, Frank,
Whose Hair hung down his Shoulders, Lank.
And followed him both Near and Far
To hear him play his Lead Guitar.
A Dream come True it was, no doubt,
The night her Hero asked her Out.
The Course of Love there is no Dodging
And, in the room where he was Lodging,
Frank worked his Mean and Loathsome Will
With great Alacrity and Skill . . .

Jayne only had herself to Thank
On Finding Frank was Fran, not Frank.

Peter Rowlett

A train from Scotland stopped one day
In country where some robbers lay.
The driver, who fulfilled his trust
And did not yield until concussed,
Received as his assessed reward
One hundred-thousandth of the hoard
He sought to cherish; while a man
Whose information helped to plan
A course towards the missing money
Received ten thousand pounds – a funny
Way to prize respective worth.
The robbers, driven then to earth,
Were greatly punished and confined
With all the cunning of a mind
Which likes to keep its prisoners taped;
But, notwithstanding, one escaped.

Dear children! Crime should not be fought
If your defence is cheaply bought.
It profits more, should life permit it,
To know about it, or commit it.

Brian Pringle

This Thing Must Be Stamped Out

(*An adventure for a modern Candide*)

It was during this sojourn in London that Candide was one day passing through a side-street off Piccadilly when he espied a gentleman standing irresolute and strained-looking. Thinking the gentleman at a loss for a place suitably to obey a demand of Nature, Candide said 'If you will accompany me, sir, I think I can resolve your difficulty.' Whereupon the man said sternly, 'So you're one of them, eh? You and me had better take a walk to the station.'

This fellow, as was revealed before the magistrate, was a detective committed to the apprehension of male prostitutes, and it was upon his evidence that Candide, though vehemently protesting, was fined Twenty Pounds.

Coming from the court, Candide remarked to Pangloss, 'Is it not strange that a kindness can be construed so evilly?'

'Not at all,' declared the Doctor, 'for the English, so swiftly yielding their other pretensions, still pride themselves on their talent for government. And where would be the need for government if mankind's instinct for kindliness and fellowship, such as your gesture expressed, were seen honestly for what it was, and given every licence? What, in such benevolent anarchy, would become of this last of the Englishman's conceits?'

John Digby

Down, Rover, Down!

(A recent avant-garde film contained a sequence in which a 'sullen' blonde was the object of a sexual assault by a dog. The film critic of the Sunday Telegraph *found this episode 'dramatically justifiable'. The usual prizes were offered for a justification, on the lines of current film criticism, of this or some comparably barbarous public spectacle)*

Could it have been done better cleaner? That is the question every serious critic must ask himself when faced with a film like *Leash-loose*, a brilliant parody of the 'anthropomorphic' school and a finely conceived parable in its own right. In this instance, Elberto Fellatio (director) reassures at once: it could not. Only a dedicated man would dare offer 90 minutes in which the sole action is the 'gang-rape' of a motherly concierge by a pack of thoroughbreds. The parody is self-evident and were this the *raison d'être* of this film, would not wholly justify it. The real art lies in the symbolism; each dog in turn represents a single facet of human experience – the woman's finally maternal response to the Peke, the touch of knockabout farce in the encounter with the Dachshund and the culminating tragedy of the Great Dane. But what at last quelled all doubts about the true value of this work was the rapidity with which *boredom* set in, how soon I was overwhelmed with a sense of futility. Who called Fellatio 'The Samuel Beckett of the Silver Screen'?

Peter Rowlett

1965

A Sad Case

(A modern social worker reports on a Shakespeare Character)

KING LEAR
from Family and Kinship in East Wessex

I met Case 349 K.L. (previously unemployed) in an entirely non-residential area of the Green Belt where he lived a semi-nomadic existence. He was a typical example of the breakdown of the Extended Family, and of those beyond reach of the Welfare State. His previous position had not made him eligible for any form of pension, and untypically his children had remained within the original familial community while he had been rehoused further out. His one-room dwelling was shared with a former employee whom he disparagingly called 'a fool', but I often found the latter more sensible. With difficulty I established that K.L.'s youngest daughter had emigrated, and an inter-generation communication failure was very marked. He had tried living with each of his two elder daughters but his inability to accept environmental change at an advanced age, and their intolerance of his hobbies, had led to a co-residential collapse. Their acquisition of his property and capital, to avoid death duties, had accelerated his present decline, of which the most disturbing feature was distinct paranoiac tendencies. I was urging immediate rehabilitation when sudden adverse weather conditions made me terminate the interview abruptly.

J. E. Crooks

I Shut My Eyes Tight
And Thought Of The Empire

(The above, said to have been uttered by Mrs. (as she had very recently become) Stanley Baldwin, reminds us of 'A lady does not move', an apophthegm attributed to Lord Curzon. But was the latter ever said, and to whom, and under what circumstances? Competitors were asked to provide a plausible answer)

As I recall, it was at one of those long Kedleston house parties in the Summer of '05 or perhaps '06, that the Marquis made his famous observation. It had been raining without respite for much of the Saturday and as the afternoon wore on, charades and theatricals, to say nothing of practical jokes, began to pall from an excess of repetition. More out of boredom than anything else, someone suggested a debate and the company were immediately seized with enthusiasm. What was more, the Marquis himself consented to act as the Speaker. Accordingly the debate began but almost before the House had left 'private business' a young American woman rose, a girl of the period in every way and without doubt educated at Ann Arbor or Vassar or some such Yankee seminary. 'I wish to make a motion', she said, unaware that such idioms cannot be imported with impunity. Long and loud was the laughter that greeted this gaffe until finally and appropriately the Marquis administered the necessary procedural rebuke without repeating the atrocity. 'A lady does not move,' he said.

D. F. Juniper

Let's Not Rest Awhile

(A description of an unrefreshing place of refreshment)

THE BLOODY FIDDLERS

Managed by Gerald (he's a card) and his wife Denise (known locally as 'Dropper'). A converted medieval abattoir on the peri-

phery of the Aston Martin country. Vehicles above 3½ litres wel-
comed on the forecourt. Mini-Coopers and Lambrettas advised to
park in the paddock behind the bogs.

Bar One: Bentleys, Bristols and Lagondas.

Chummy. Splendid place to recover from the ravages of board
meetings. Gerald will oblige with filthy stories for customers
ordering John Collinses and plates of smoked-salmon sandwiches.
Denise available Thursday afternoons (country-cottage perform-
ances only).

Bar Two: Jags, Triumphs and Yankee jobs.

Cosy. Lonely male drinkers addressed by Denise as "darling".
Gerald will provide cleaner stories about Harold Wilson if per-
suaded to 'have one'. Denise occasionally possible Monday morn-
ings (back-seats considered).

Bar Three: Austins, Fords and Vauxhalls.

Comfortable. Great respect accorded. Sir or Madam terms. Gerald
will twirl handlebar-moustache pleasantly. Denise will nod graciously but quietly decline invitations ('I'll pretend I never heard that,
sir').

Bar Four: Bangers, bicycles and bipeds.

Crowded. Gerald ('Why don't you try the place up the road, cock?'),
Denise ('Git aht ev it, yer dirty ole bleeder').

Russell Lucas

The Thing's Obvious

(*Moscow Radio interpreted the Great Train Robbery as a British
secret service fund-raising project. Prizes were offered for a communist
interpretation of other famous criminal activities*)

from THE ORACLE, a monthly Albanian newsletter.

One of the most vigilant secrets of the notorious English Establish-
ment Club is ultimately out!! The real alias of the murderer Jack
Ripper. It is – you can knock him down with a feather – the mad
Scotchman, Sir Lloyd George!!! It was the old beastial ghoul
Gladstone, known to all as 'GOM', who, already much infamed for

debouching the strumpots of Soho into the parlour of his wife, led the young man, his passions much inflamated by the Methodical repressions of his native valley, the Gorbals, down into the Lime-house, where he made speeches and was bundling off many boat-loads of our heroic Chinese brothren, much indigenous there, to be 'Coolies' in Rhodesia. Then he, Sir Lloyd, would strut back rollick-ing into the foggy White Chapel of Belgravia, stripping and ripping the womanhood as he would. It was Churchill, who as Homcs Secretary, nosed out the murky conundrum in all its dirty linen and blackballed Sir Lloyd into being 'front guy' of the Cabinet, of which he, Churchill, was pulling the strings. And it was too Churchill in 1940, who sent in the posses of strong-arm dynamiters to East London, where tokens of the outrageousness still loitered, to blow it up in the smithereens, blaming it all on damn bombage from air raids, which Comrade Stalin proved were never taking place and which was just an excusing for not going in on the Second Front. So there you have it, as the idiom is going, in a nutcase!!

Martin Fagg

Sandy Douglas-Home

(*It has been suggested that Sir Alec Douglas-Home's favourite author may be John Buchan. Another theory is that Sir Alec does not really exist, but is simply a projection of the late John Buchan's imagination. Competitors contrived an episode from the unpublished Richard Hannay novel in which Sandy Douglas-Home makes his first appearance*)

London and August are not made for one another and I was feeling like a fish out of water. Fosse had been lent to some newly-married Wymondham cousins, Mary was yachting with the Turpins, and Peter John had gone off mole-watching with Sir Arthur and David Wharncliffe in the Blaskets. I was kicking my heels in a strange club while my own was closed for cleaning. By rights, I should have been shooting Archie Roylance's grouse, but the birds were all diseased; Archie was out for the blood of the Minister of Agriculture, who'd been spraying the moors with some new-fangled insecticide. I was yawning my head off over *Blackwood's* when: 'Dick, you sly old devil! You're ahead of time!' I was never more pleased to hear Burminster's genial boom.

He tugged at the bell-pull and sank into the chair beside me. 'Dick, there's hell's own broth brewing...' He broke off as a waitress came for his order. 'Two Boobies.' 'Yes, your Grace.' The voice had a curious sibilance, and I was looking after her as she moved away with the lithe grace of a boy when a page brought me a telegram. 'For you, Sir Richard.' I was startled to catch a wink from an eye as clear as a Kudu's. As I watched him leave the room with the graceful litheness of a girl, Burminster's rich chuckle broke the silence. 'You've got it, Dick!' 'You mean – Sandy?' He nodded. 'Then who's the other one?' 'She's called Sandy, too. Or rather, he is. Sandy found her – him, I mean – somewhere back of the Cheviots. The Douglas boy. First-class stuff. Now listen, Dick, and I'll put you in the picture. I don't suppose you've heard of a half-baked peace movement called UN...'

John Davenport

I Was Too Young
At The Time To Understand Why
My Mother Was Crying

(*Extracts from competitors' autobiographies which were to be as cliché-studded as possible*)

Though Cobbins long ago fell to the demolition men, in that glorious summer of 1939 it stood proudly unaware of the storm so soon to sweep it away and, with it, a whole way of life. It was there I first met Alethea.

I had motored over from Cambridge in time to hear the first tinkle of china which augured the ritual of afternoon tea in the Long Gallery. Dawkins, my aunt's butler, destined for a hero's death at Dunkirk, opened the door and there beside the Adam fireplace, in a shaft of sunlight, I saw the most beautiful face I had ever seen.

What was said as we took tea and toyed with the dainty pink cakes, supplied daily by Gunter's, I cannot recall, but, later, in the evening's cool, Alethea and I strolled out to the gazebo, high above the ornamental lake. This Palladian temple, constructed by my grandfather who combined with the hard-headedness of a successful ironfounder a rare taste and imagination, was the perfect setting for Alethea's classical beauty. Neither of us spoke but each knew what was in the mind of the other as she came towards me. Her grave lips warmed into that smile of which not even a cruel German bomb was able to rob me, for Alethea passed it on to Felicity as perhaps her richest legacy of all.

Lyndon Irving

1966

May I Add A Word?

(God is alive, it has been whispered, and is living in Argentina. But if He is dead, He rates an obituary)

JC writes: The generous obituary of my father which appeared in yesterday's *Times* rightly emphasised his achievements in construction and maintenance, and the many legal precedents which he established in his judicial capacity. What is not so generally known, however, is that my father took a keen personal interest in several charities. Believing as he did that the only true wealth lies in moral worth, he was anxious to do all he could for the morally under-privileged and the ethically deprived. He knew full well that no amount of mere dross could ever compensate for the profound distress caused by personal dishonesty, cruelty, greed and a ruthless hunger for power. He did believe, however, that this trivial and, as it might seem, almost insulting compensation should at least be *offered* to those of the poor who were prepared to accept it. I know that it was a great and constant source of satisfaction to my father that so many of these tragically destitute men and women were willing to accept these token compensations of material wealth and power.

Philip Toynbee

Sincerest Forms of Flattery

(*Competitors were asked for a parody of the contemporary writer whom they judged most eligible for parody*)

C. P. SNOW

Paunceley was regaling us with the clarets of '56.

'This is very civil of you, Senior Tutor,' observed Mainwaring.

'Thank you, Professor of Palaeontology and Sometime Fellow of Jesus,' replied Paunceley. He seemed nervous, drawn, tense.

It was a languorous February night, heady with the rich evocative reek of sweet-william. The chrysanthemums blazed in the court, a Scotch mist draped the plane-trees and above, in the sky, shimmered the stars – countless, desolate, shining.

I felt increasingly uneasy about my tendency to fire off adjectives in threes. It was compulsive, embarrassing, ineluctable; but at least it fostered the illusion of a mind that was diamond-sharp, incisive, brilliant.

'I have asked you to come here before breakfast,' continued Paunceley, 'because I have a most unsavoury revelation to make to you about one of your colleagues.'

I glanced at Grimsby-Browne. He seemed suddenly immensely old, haggard, shrivelled. Had he committed the unforgivable and falsified a footnote? I studied Basingstoke, the Bursar. He too seemed suddenly bowed, broken, desiccated. Had he done the unspeakable and embezzled the battels? The scent of Old Man's Beard saturated the combination room.

'It concerns Charles Snow,' said Paunceley.

The tension was now unbearably taut, torturing, tense. The plangent aroma of montbretia seemed to pervade every electron of my being.

The Senior Tutor's tone was dry, aloof, Olympian.

'I have discovered that his real name is Godfrey Winn.'

Martin Fagg

TED WILLIS

A darkened bedroom. The light is suddenly switched on by Mrs Friday, in bed.

Mrs Friday: Hello, who are you?
Chalky White: I'm Chalky White. I've come to half-inch your tom.
Mrs Friday: Fancy!
Chalky: Shut your north-and-south. Where is it?
Mrs Friday: Well, I never. You're a cool one and no mistake, I
shouldn't wonder.
Sergeant Dockgreen enters.
Dockgreen: Chuck it, Chalky.
Mrs Friday: Well, knock on any door!
Dockgreen: Sorry to trouble you, Mrs F. It's the flowery dell for
you, my lad.
Chalky: I ain't done nothing. Straight up.
Dockgreen: That's as maybe.
Mrs Friday: Give him a Russian dance, Sarge. They do say it takes
all sorts. What would you say to a nice cuppa?
Dockgreen: (*facing front*) We get all kinds in the manor. Some are
good 'uns and some are bad 'uns. Chalky was one of the lucky
ones. He's going straight now, thanks to Mrs Friday. Which
only goes to show – it's dangerous over-taking on a hill.

Roger Woddis

Once Again Assembled Here

(*Competitors, invited to comment in verse on the horrors of a Reunion
Dinner, chose Betjeman as their model and did not stint the creaking
trusses, clicking dentures and Brown Windsor soup*)

Blaggard Major, Hogget Minor, Soddom Minimus and Leach –
Bloods and bullies, duds and bounders, fill the room with drunken
speech;
Shouting in prolonged crescendo what success they've made of
Life;
Smothering schoolboy indiscretions with a lawful wedded wife.
Oh, what ridicule and shame
Lurks behind each brutish name!

Hawkes (who could not add two digits) buys and sells Algerian wine.
Goving (once the Fourth Form sadist) owns a North Rhodesian
mine.
Heckendorff (whose only pleasure was to drill the O.T.C.)
Helps his uncle who is something in the gaming industry.
    Lord dismiss us with Thy curse,
    Who have made a bad thing worse.

Gerald Priestland

A Personal Appearance

(An extract from a modern John Aubrey)

Being hard-prest for a debt of 200 *li*, I was prevayled upon to
take parte in a publick discussione got up for the Televizione. Old
Oxonian Freinds have counselled me often to doe this, they having
founde it a most excellent way for a scholarely man to make moneye.
I met with a Mr Andrewes, who took me somewhat aback by saying
he would not have me talke of historikal matters, or of bookes and
learnynge, since those watching the Entertaynment would be more
disposed to lyke Joakes of a lewde nature, though Mr Andrewes
himselfe confesst he was not of that minde.

I consented with some apprehention to appeare, though I was
much chagrined to hear it put about that I was a famous Gossipe.
At the studioe I came upon others that were to joyne in the Conversations, among them persons of Tytle, who amazed me with their
behaviour, appearing to be no little in drinke; also a raskal with long
haire, a singer of sortes, with an Estate among the richest in England.

I was myselfe given royal entertaynment, and on the conversation
starting I tolde a storye or two, which pleased some mightilye but
drewe harsh words from Mrs Whyte House, who is sett up to judge
what is good for the People; also Mr Andrewes, I feare, somewhat
out of humour with me.

Peter Veale

Sussex By The Sea

(Kipling on the Glyndebourne Festival)

In their Rollses and their Jags, in their very gladdest rags,
They're a-pourin' through the Sussex countryside,
For there's music in the air and they want their annual share
Of Op'ra with some champers on the side.
Yes, the kids are safe with nanny so it's off to *Don Giovanni*
For a classy bloomin' operatic fling.
Oh, there's nothing rag-and-taggy or the least bit Cav-and-Paggy
Down at Glyndebourne where the Christie minstrels sing.

Come the end of ev'ry May there's a call the toffs obey
To mix a bit of culture with their class,
And so you find them there in the balmy Sussex air
A-listenin' and a-strollin' on the grass.
They leave *La Traviata* to the lower social strata
And a Glyndebourne *Butterfly* just isn't done,
But if your cup of tea is stuff like *Dido and Aeneas*
Better put your black tie on and join the fun.

Peter Veale

Advice Is Seldom Welcome

(Part of a letter from a modern Lord Chesterfield to his son)

. . . This idea of yours of swopping schools is bonkers. As if Holland
Park would take you at 17. It just isn't true that I resent your not
getting into Pop. *I* did, admittedly – but you clearly lack my charm.
What *does* irritate me is your describing your Housemaster as an
absolute shit. Of *course* the man's an absolute shit. He was that when
I was at the place and the intervening 20 years can only have ripened
his bouquet. God knows what sort of a career you're going to have
in the City if you start being so damned fussy about who you mix
with.

I don't want to nag, old boy, but there *is* just one other thing. You know I don't mind your using the Jag when you're at home – even if you do seem to have buggered the clutch. But *please*, Jimbo, *don't* stuff used contraceptives in the dashboard. That sort of thing is really *frightfully* bad form, as well as desperately insan. Your mother was fishing around in there for her National Trust bloody handbook and . . . She was *rather* choked.

Tim O'Dowda

Sequel

(*A sequel to Nell Dunn's* Up the Junction)

UP THE NAVE

The church is a dirty grey in the early morning sun, the walls scabby with moss. The vestry door creaks when I open it.

'Looking for someone ?'

'Just dropped in for a chat, vicar.'

He is thirtyish, tired-looking, with a face like a beat-up Buick.

'Have a fag.' He pushes over a cracked plastic pouch and a packet of papers. I roll myself a cigarette, squatting on the floor amid a pile of faded prayer-books. 'I'm just finishing off the parish mag. Waste of time, really. The curate uses it for bog-paper.'

'How's business ?'

'Shocking. Nobody reckons God these days.'

He bends down to pick up a sheet of paper off the floor, but I see his eyes travel swiftly up my exposed thigh.

'It's the groups.'

'Yes. I was thinking of starting one myself. The Meeks. Might pull them in.'

The door opens. Shoulder-length hair, black leather jacket, fag in mouth.

'Can't make choir practice this evening, vic. Got to see a bird. Says I've put her up the spout.'

He goes, whistling 'We can work it out'. We hear the roar of his bike.

The vicar shakes his head. 'Lucky sod.'

Roger Woddis

Shakespeare Foreword

(An excerpt from a preface by Shakespeare to one of his plays)

My wife, who esteems herself the most perspicacious, as she has ever proved herself the most styptick of my criticks, is greatly affected by the parlous predicament of the lady Octavia in this play, but so little moved by that of Cleopatra (that 'pert, bedizen'd slut', as she deems her) that she would, she avers, plough up with her nails the visage of any person analagouse to her that she ever discover'd in my compagnye. But my wife entertains but small regard for the play at large, for on my concluding the reading of it to her in bed by rushlight (as is my wont), she did fetch a mightye yawn and cry: 'A miss, a miss, a palpable miss! There was never yet an audience that would stomack a play with fortie scenes that leapeth aboute from playce to playce like a flea on a pedlar's rumpe.' Whereupon the froward creature did straightway address herself to a heavy and sonorous sleepe. There is, I must owne, some substance in her objection. It seemeth that I did, in the act of inditing my play, conjecture means by which the brief visions of which my drama is made up mighte be woven into some continuous skein, impress'd upon some delicate yet durable film . . .

Tim O'Dowda

1967

Compulsive Viewing

(*The television programme* Man Alive *has taken to advertising in* The Times *agony column for people willing to confess in front of cameras. Competitors were invited to submit letters in reply calculated to bring the programme producer hurrying to their doors*)

Dear Man Alive,
    It all started at 8.55 p.m. on 11 September 1965 on ITV. I realised I was in love with Reginald Bosanquet. Next day I left my wife and eight children determined to accept my true nature. Being coloured I had great difficulty finding lodgings in London – especially as I needed large rooms to house all my 'apparatus'. When I contacted Mr Bosanquet I was horrified to find that he did not reciprocate my passion. Then, finding myself uninterested in other men, I became an alcoholic. During this period of heavy drinking I first noticed the 'change'. I was then forced to steal money for the fare to Copenhagen. I returned to get a job as a strip-tease artiste in a London club. I am now engaged to the club manager. As he is coloured our marriage will not be without difficulties as I am now white (an optional extra in Copenhagen). However, I am happy for the first time, and all thanks to Reginald Bosanquet – my Bosie. I am left-handed and have an irrational fear of tortoises.

Stanley Price

Misleading Information
For Tourists Visiting London

(This subject, a great favourite with competitors, is set at regular intervals)

Women are not allowed upstairs on buses; if you see a woman there, ask her politely to descend.

David Gordon

Prostitutes are now seen only occasionally. On certain days, however, they come out in force, easily recognised by the little favours they sell from trays.

P. W. R. Foot

All foreigners have the privilege of watching cricket matches from in front of the large white screens, to help them learn the finer points of the game. Both players and spectators will acknowledge your arrival with waves and shouts of greeting.

J. M. Crooks

Visitors in London hotels are expected by the management to hang the bed-linen out of the windows to air.

Axel Castle

Try the famous echo in the British Museum Reading Room.

Gerard Hoffnung

On first entering an Underground train, it is customary to shake hands with every passenger.

R. J. Phillips

If you take a taxi, the driver will be only too willing to give your shoes a polish while waiting at the traffic-lights.

R. J. Phillips

In the interests of hygiene you should spray your taxi, train, bus or Underground seat with an antiseptic deodorant.

W. A. Payne

Yellow lines painted on roads indicate the number of rows of parking permitted.

Joan Hymans

Pine Trees Are Tall
But They Do Not Reach The Sky

(*Competitors furnished handy, meaningless proverbs for all occasions*)

It's a weak plaice that can't swim.

Rhoda Tuck Pook

Sick yaks leave light tracks.

P. Clifton

A shirt has a tail but cannot bark.

Douglas Hawson

A starving dog can still carry fleas.

W. E. Webb

The melting snow hates not the sun.

Ron Rubin

No leg's too short to reach the ground.

Lyndon Irving

Death is free but it costs you your life.

R. Rossetti

136

Now He Tells Us

(*It was felt that De Gaulle would not rest on his Canadian laurels for long and a newspaper report was asked for of the next international incident stirred up by the General*)

The General's announcement, in the course of his nationwide broadcast last night, that he is in fact Jesus Christ, has caused remarkably little stir in the capital. It is felt that as his actions have for such a long time now been intelligible only on such a basis of belief, his disclosure of his divine provenance merely adds official confirmation to a *de facto* assumption. Reports of what occurred at the preliminary cabinet meeting are still incomplete, but M. Couve de Murville is said to have received the news with his usual glacial urbanity, while if a momentary flicker of M. Pompidou's luxuriant eyebrows betrayed certain slight reservations on his part, he was wise enough not to voice them. Speculation here centres on the nature of the reply that the Pope is likely to make to the General's summons to him as his Vicar to come to Paris to report, reverentially, on his stewardship.

Tim O'Dowda

By-The-By

(*Mary McCarthy has pointed out that one can learn how to make strawberry jam from reading* Anna Karenina. *Other great masterpieces may be similarly helpful*)

Exponents of the art of flower arrangement, always on the search for stimulating variations, may find D. H. Lawrence's *Lady Chatterley's Lover* most exciting reading. Mr Lawrence's suggestions for making use of forget-me-nots and campions will delight you. Read this book and learn from it. You may discover a whole new world in your potting shed.

R. Goode

The Bible is full of useful hints. What better tip for a hostess than to bring forth butter in a lordly dish, or keep inferior wine to the last? After the shops have closed, who would have thought of rubbing an ear of corn, looking for honey in a dead lion, or munching a locust? There are hints on savoir faire: what to do when caught naked, what to cook for a prodigal son, what wise virgins do. Then in a tight spot, how unexpected, but how effective, the jawbone of an ass, or a tent peg. And don't forget a Bible worn over the heart has stopped many a bullet.

Party tricks abound. Do you want to act hairy? Astound your girl-friend! Ask her to close her eyes and have a feel . . . There's boat-building and many construction jobs for do-it-yourself enthusiasts; also home doctor remedies like wine for cuts and a simple cure for leprosy. For the bedside, The Song of Solomon is not the only tale that makes exciting reading, and hippies out of LSD swear by Revelations. Here indeed is a vade-mecum.

T. Griffiths

Index

*The page numbers in the Index refer to the page on which the competitors'
names appear, not the page on which their pieces start.*

GEORGE ALLEN & UNWIN LTD

London: 40 Museum Street, W.C.1

Auckland: P.O. Box 36013, Northcote Central N.4
Barbados: P.O. Box 222, Bridgetown
Bombay: 15 Graham Road, Ballard Estate, Bombay 1
Buenos Aires: Escritorio 454–459, Florida 165
Beirut: Deeb Building, Jeanne d'Arc Street
Calcutta: 17 Chittaranjan Avenue, Calcutta 13
Cape Town: 68 Shortmarket Street
Hong Kong: 105 Wing On Mansion, 26 Hancow Road, Kowloon
Ibadan: P.O. Box 62
Karachi: Karachi Chambers, McLeod Road
Madras: Mohan Mansions, 38c Mount Road, Madras 6
Mexico: Villalongin 32, Piso, Mexico 5, D.F.
Nairobi: P.O. Box 30583
New Delhi: 13–14 Asaf Ali Road, New Delhi 1
Ontario: 81 Curlew Drive, Don Mills
Philippines: P.O. Box 4322, Manila
Rio de Janeiro: Caixa Postal 2537–Zc–00
Singapore: 36c Prinsep Street, Singapore 7
Sydney N.S.W.: Bradbury House, 55 York Street
Tokyo: P.O. Box 26, Kamata

BY BASIL BOOTHROYD

Let's Stay Married

You could kill your husband about three times a week, but love him just the same? Your wife regularly drives you out of your mind, but you adore her still? The laughter in these pages is specially for you.

And even more so if, as the trend towards easier divorce gets trendier, you'll be rushing off to the lawyers every time the game of *Matrimony* (Fun for all the Family) falls short of the picture on the lid. 'My client alleges, my Lord, that she was telling her husband an extraordinary dream she'd had, when he left her for the station whistling.' 'Decree granted. Next?'

Basil Boothroyd, known to more than a quarter of a century's *Punch* readers as a man of sunny disposition, views these possibilities with concern—but examines them uproariously. He believes that every future bride and groom should find a copy of this book among their wedding presents. If not, their first duty of the honeymoon is to give one to each other.

With 400,000 marriages a year in the UK alone, says Boothroyd, this should push *Let's Stay Married* into a second edition in no time.

Might save lots of marriages, too.

You Can't Be Serious

Basil Boothroyd is as widely known through his broadcasts as through his regular weekly *Punch* articles. Whether in print or on the air his 'voice' is individual and unmistakable. It has the insuppressible chuckle that speaks of a desperate acceptance of life's absurdities, humiliations and plain downright obstructionism: all these are the common experience, but Boothroyd's special gift is to see them through laugh-coloured glasses. Not only that, but to lend these invaluable aids to his readers, thus correcting what might be a grey and astigmatic view of our times. *You Can't Be Serious* collects a sparkling selection of his recent *Punch* pieces. The title, and the author, speak for themselves.

LONDON · GEORGE ALLEN & UNWIN LTD